How to Pass FCE

First Certificate in English

Exam practice in Reading

Brian Orpet

Contents

Introduction 1

This book will be of use to students who are preparing on their own for the new Cambridge First Certificate Examination in English and also to students in schools or colleges who wish to have extra practice material.

The book explains what the four parts of this paper consist of and gives suggestions on how candidates should approach the different parts of this paper. There are Practice Exercises which lead students to Exam Exercises. The Practice Exercises are shorter and easier than in the First Certificate, and build up the necessary skills. The Exam Exercises are not arranged in order of difficulty but are all at First Certificate level and the same length as in the exam. There are in addition two full Trial Papers at the end of the book.

Answers to all the Practice Exercises and Exam Exercises, with notes to explain answers, are given in *Answers and Notes* on page 64.

The book will help students to become familiar with Paper 1 and will give them confidence in taking the examination. It should, however, be made clear that this is *not* a course book.

USING THE BOOK

Different students will find different ways of using the book. Some students who feel confident on one or two parts of the paper may ignore those parts and concentrate on the other parts. Other students may wish to work simply on the practice material and to ignore the explanations in each part.

Most students will benefit from studying each part of the book in turn and doing two of the four Exam Exercises in each part. When students have completed all four parts they should try to do the remaining Exam Exercises and, finally, the two full Trial Papers.

TRIAL PAPERS

The two full papers are called Trial Papers. To gain full value from these, students should work through them under examination conditions, that is taking the correct length of time and not referring to any books whilst doing them. There is an answer sheet at the back of the book (see page 84) which students may use to write answers on, as would happen in the actual examination.

The Exam Exercises in the different parts of the book are all of First Certificate level and students may, if they wish, make up extra Trial Papers by putting together the Exam Exercises from the four different parts.

Before doing the Trial Papers it is a good idea to look at the section for each part of the test called **Doing the test** and **Remember**.

MARKS

In all parts every answer is worth 1 mark. In order to pass the First Certificate Examination, you need to reach an overall mark of about 60% across the 5 papers. You should aim, therefore, to gain 60% on the Trial Papers in this book (that is about 21 marks).

FILLING IN THE ANSWER SHEET

On the answer sheet you will see question numbers from 1 to 35. At the side of each number are the letters **A**, **B**, **C**, **D**, **E**, **F**, **G**, **H**, **I**. Underneath each letter is a small box. When you have chosen an answer, you must make a mark **in pencil** in the appropriate box.

For example, if you decide that the correct answer for question 8 is B, you mark the answer sheet in the way shown below.

You must never mark more than any one letter for an answer. If you do this, your answer will definitely be wrong. If you change your mind about an answer, remember to rub out the answer you first thought of before putting in the new answer.

It may seem strange that there are nine letters (**A**, **B**, **C**, **D**, **E**, **F**, **G**, **H**, **I**) on your answer sheet even though there may be a smaller number of answers to choose from on the question paper. Do not worry about this as this is simply a standard form. Not all the parts of the paper have all these possible answers to choose from – in Part 2, for instance, you will have only four choices for each question, so your answer will have to be **A**, **B**, **C** or **D**.

Pencil

In the examination all answers must be written on the answer sheet in pencil. The Centre where you are taking the examination may provide you with a pencil for the test but it is a good idea to take a pencil of your own in case the centre does not give you one. It is also sensible to bring with you a rubber to rub out any answers which you wish to change.

TIME

You will have 1 hour and 15 minutes to do this paper. Generally, it is best to work through the paper in the order of the parts (that is Part 1 first, Part 2 second, and so on). However, if you have always found one part far more difficult than the other parts, it may be a good idea to leave this until the end.

When you do the Trial Papers, you should get an idea of how long to spend on the different parts of the paper. Below is a *suggestion* of how long to spend on these parts:

Part 1: 15 minutes
Part 2: 20 minutes
Part 3: 15 minutes
Part 4: 20 minutes
Revision: 5 minutes

Remember these times are *only suggestions* and they will not be suitable for everyone. You may well spend more time on parts which you find difficult and less time on parts you find easy. Doing the Trial Papers should help you to organise your time in the most suitable way for you.

Exam tip

One of the best ways of improving your marks in this paper is to read as much as you can. Read magazines, books, newspapers – everything you can find written in English. The more you read, the more you will understand.

LOOKING AT PART 1

As you read this, look at page 8 for an example. In this part of the test you have a number of short phrases or sentences followed by a passage which is split into several paragraphs. At the beginning of each paragraph there will be a number (1, 2, 3, etc.) in a box.

The short phrases or sentences before the passage will give you either a heading (or title) for each paragraph or a summary of each paragraph. Each phrase or sentence will have a letter (A, B, C, etc.) in front of it. You must choose one of these phrases or sentences to go with each paragraph. For example, if you read a passage and think that the best summary or heading for the third paragraph is phrase B, you must mark B on your answer sheet at the side of number 3.

The correct answer for the first paragraph (which always has the figure 0 at the beginning) is always given for you as an example of what to do, so be careful not to put the answer for 0 as your first answer. Note also that there will always be at least one of the phrases which does not fit with any paragraph.

What you have to do in this test is to try to decide what is the main point being made in the paragraph, as this is what will appear in the heading or the summary. Sometimes you will see a word appearing in a heading or summary which appears in just one of the paragraphs. For example you might see that heading D contains the word *satisfaction* and that this word is also in paragraph 2 but not in any other paragraph. *Do not think* that it is certain, therefore, that heading D must go with paragraph 2; this may or may not be the case – you must read the whole of the heading and the paragraph before you decide on an answer.

PRACTICE EXERCISES

Exercises 1-6

In order to help you to become used to choosing titles or summaries to go with a paragraph, the first six exercises consist of a single paragraph for which there is a choice of headings or summaries.

PRACTICE EXERCISE 1

Which of the following phrases provides the best heading for the passage?

A No more village football
B New date for match to be fixed
C Illness halts football match
D Whole Cotville team hit by colds

The annual football match between the villages of Hamden and Cotville has had to be cancelled because most members of the Cotville team are suffering from heavy colds. As it is so late in the season, it seems unlikely that a new date for the match can be arranged.

Now check your answer on page 64.

PRACTICE EXERCISE 2

Which of the following sentences gives the best summary of the passage?

A Edinburgh is a really interesting place to visit.
B On no account should you miss visiting Edinburgh Castle.
C It is a problem finding things to do in Edinburgh.
D It is not difficult to see all of Edinburgh in a short time.

Edinburgh is full of places of interest and one of the problems for a visitor with only a short time at his or her disposal is what to see. Many would choose Edinburgh Castle, with its marvellous views of the city, whilst others would want to walk down the Royal Mile to visit the Palace of Holyrood House. Still others might simply choose to go shopping on the famous Princes Street.

Now check your answer on page 64.

PRACTICE EXERCISE 3

Which of the following phrases provides the best heading for the passage?

A Local musical contest
B Orchestra's first time in London
C Brandon hoping to win again
D Away for the weekend

Members of the Brandon School orchestra are looking forward to their visit to London next weekend, when they will be taking part in a competition for youth orchestras from all over Britain. This will be the third time they have entered the contest; although they have never won any prizes, the members of the orchestra always enjoy their weekend away.

Now check you answer on page 64.

PRACTICE EXERCISE 4

Which of the following sentences gives the best summary of the passage?

A It is impossible to stay in a top class hotel without spending a lot of money.
B All top class hotels offer rooms at cheaper rates at weekends.
C Top class hotels are never used by business travellers at weekends.
D Rooms in some top class hotels cost less at weekends.

Visiting different parts of Britain can be an expensive business if you want to stay in top class hotels. However, many hotels that cater for business travellers on generous expense accounts during the week drop their rates at weekends, when there are some surprisingly good bargains to be found.

Now check your answer on page 64.

PRACTICE EXERCISE 5

Which of the following phrases provides the best heading for the passage?

A Doctor fails to visit patient
B A phone proves its value
C Doctor rescued from farm
D Rescue services arrive too late

A doctor was trapped in his car last night by the snow. He had been visiting a patient who lived on an isolated farm, but having driven a few kilometres, found it impossible to continue because the snow was too thick on the road. Fortunately, he had a mobile phone in the car and was able to contact the rescue services, who managed to reach him a few hours later.

Now check your answer on page 64.

PRACTICE EXERCISE 6

Which of the following sentences gives the best summary of the passage?

A Emergency teams are trying to prevent oil escaping from a factory.
B Oil for making toffee has escaped into the River Medway.
C Efforts are being made to save a river from pollution.
D Most of the oil is on the banks of the river.

There was a threat of major pollution of the River Medway near Tonbridge in Kent last night, when hundreds of gallons of oil escaped from a factory on the banks of the river. Emergency teams have been called in to fight the pollution. The river was described as looking like 'liquid toffee'.

Now check your answer on page 64.

Exercises 7 and 8

In the following two exercises, each passage consists of two paragraphs.

PRACTICE EXERCISE 7

Choose the most suitable heading for each of the two paragraphs below from the following phrases.

A Club for all writers
B An even better service
C Enthusiastic reception
D Hoping for more requests
E Chance for discussion
F Total success

1 The Deansgate Literary Club was established several years ago with the aim of establishing a centre where people who love books could listen to leading authors and personalities, meet people who share their enthusiasm and talk about the latest publications in a friendly and relaxed atmosphere. We trust that we have fulfilled at least some of these aims.

2 The coming year promises to be another exciting year for publications and new authors. We intend to make sure that our visiting novelists, biographers, poets, politicians, stars and personalities represent the best talents of the current literary scene. We also hope that with an improved information system your requests will be dealt with more effectively.

Now check your answers on page 64.

PRACTICE EXERCISE 8

Choose the most suitable summary for each of the two paragraphs below from the following sentences.

A Rather more people are travelling between Manchester and Basle than expected.
B More frequent flights will be introduced on the route after a year.
C There have rarely been empty seats on the flights in the evening.
D Very few people are flying from Manchester to Basle in the morning.
E It may eventually be possible to have more flights on the route.
F Far more people are using these flights than had been expected.

1 Passenger numbers for the first three months of Crossair's service between Manchester and Basle are slightly above expectation. Moritz Suter, the airline chairman, said that the evening flights, especially, were doing very well and that it was hoped that numbers on the morning service would soon increase.

2 During November and December some 1,800 people per month used the new service with, on average, 40% of the seats being filled. Suter added, "We are pretty satisfied for the present with the route's development. If, after a year, the present progress has been maintained, we shall consider increasing frequency."

Now check your answers on page 65.

Exercises 9 and 10

In the following two exercises, each passage consists of three paragraphs.

PRACTICE EXERCISE 9

Choose the most suitable heading for each of the three paragraphs below from the following phrases.

A Hospital to blame
B Checking on comments
C Lack of communication
D Inaccurate use of language
E Not realising others are present
F Heard in the lift
G Too much talk in private

1 Researchers made 250 journeys in lifts in five hospitals in Pittsburg in the USA to see if staff were making unpleasant remarks about patients without realising that relatives of patients might be standing next to them.

2 One doctor was heard to say that a patient's death was the hospital's fault. A nurse said that one of her colleagues must have been drunk the previous evening. Some staff made nasty comments about patients and their families, in one case criticising the clothes they wore.

3 Professor Peter Ubel of the University of Pennsylvania, who was in charge of the project, said that people easily forget that they are in a public place. "Many conversations start in the privacy of an office and continue into the corridor and into the lift."

Now check your answers on page 65.

PRACTICE EXERCISE 10

Choose the most suitable summary for each of the three paragraphs below from the following sentences.

A The shop will continue to offer bargains after the first day.
B You cannot buy anything apart from phones in the shop.
C All phones will be sold at half price on the first day.
D It will be easy to phone if you go to the shop regularly.
E If you pay a little extra for a phone, making phone calls will be cheaper.
F Many customers on the first day will be able to buy phones cheaply.
G You will not be forced to buy a phone if you ask for advice in the shop.

1 When our shop opens on 20th May, you'll find we have a lot to offer. As a shop dedicated to selling phones, there will be a wide range of the best products on display. To celebrate our opening, the first hundred customers to buy any phone will pay only half the marked price.

2 If you are unable to take advantage of our 'half price phone' offer, don't worry as there will be other offers in the near future. As well as new phones, the shop will feature many extra items to make phoning easier and cheaper.

3 To make sure that you understand how we can help you, there will always be experienced and highly trained staff on hand to answer any questions and to give advice without obligation. Make sure you visit us regularly to see how we can make phoning even easier and cheaper for you.

Now check your answers on page 65.

DOING THE EXAM

1 First of all, read through the headings (or summaries) as these will give you an idea of what the passage is about.

2 Then read through the whole of the passage but do *not* begin to choose the phrases which are most suitable for the various paragraphs.

3 Read through the phrases again. Note which phrase is given to you as the example to go with the first paragraph. Cross this answer out on the question paper so that you do not keep looking at it when you are wanting to find other answers.

4 You may already feel that you know which phrases should go with some of the paragraphs. If this is so, read the appropriate paragraphs and, if you think your choice is correct, mark it on your answer sheet.

5 When you have chosen a heading (or summary), cross it out lightly on the question paper so that you do not keep looking at it. (However, do not cross the words out too heavily as you may later decide that answer was wrong and you may wish to look at it again.)

6 Now read through the first paragraph for which you have not yet chosen a phrase. Read through the phrases carefully and try to choose the one which is most suitable for this paragraph. If you find it impossible to make a choice, move on to the next paragraph and try to find a suitable phrase for this one.

7 When you have gone through the whole of the passage, go back to any paragraphs for which you have not found a suitable phrase; there will probably be only a few phrases remaining, which should make it easier for you to choose one.

Remember

- Only one of the phrases will be suitable for each paragraph. *Never* mark more than two letters for one answer.
- One of the phrases will not be suitable for any paragraph, so that when you come to the end of this part of the paper, there will still be one phrase which you have not used.
- Do not choose a heading (or summary) to go with a paragraph simply because the heading contains a word which appears only in that paragraph. This may be the right answer but it may also be wrong. Read the whole heading and the whole paragraph.
- If you miss out an answer, make sure that when you put in the next answer, you put it by the correct number (that is to say that if, for example, you missed out answer 4, do not put answer 5 at the side of number 4).
- If you change your mind about an answer, remember to rub out the answer you had already indicated.
- Always mark one of the letters on the answer sheet even if, after thinking about the item, you are simply guessing the answer. There is always a chance that you may be right.

EXAM EXERCISES

EXAM EXERCISE 1

You are going to read an article about the effect that listening to music might have on the brain. Choose from the list **A-I** the sentence which best summarises each part (**1-7**) of the article. There is one extra sentence which you do not need to use. There is an example at the beginning (**0**).

A Pupils were put into groups to listen to different things.
B The experiment could lead to new methods of teaching.
C Pupils doing best had probably liked what they had heard.
D It was thought that difficult music made the brain work better.
E The experiment suggests that the children did not listen to Mozart.
F Listening to Mozart seemed to improve mental ability.
G Those listening to pop music did best on the test.
H The effect of music on people may be different according to age.
I The experiment was carried out in all parts of Britain.

MUSIC TO HELP YOUR BRAIN

0 | I

Listening to pop music may make you cleverer, according to a Megalab experiment in which 11,000 children in 250 schools across Britain took part.

1 |

The idea was put forward as a scientific study by Dr Sue Hallam of the Institute of Education, London, to follow up work in California which suggested that listening to music by Mozart for ten minutes had a direct effect on people's ability to work out problems.

2 |

The Megalab experiment took place at eleven o'clock one Thursday morning. School children were split at random into three separate groups: one listening to Mozart, one to a pop group and one to a conversation in which Dr Hallam discussed Megalab.

3 |

The children were then given problem-solving tasks. The group which had listened to the discussion scored 52 per cent, those who had listened to Mozart also scored 52 per cent, but those who had listened to the pop group scored 56 per cent. Dr Hallam said the result is interesting and 'approaching significance'.

4 |

She thought that the reason was not due to the 'Mozart effect' but because the mood of the children had changed, so they were more aroused and tried harder. 'They were probably enjoying it and so they were well motivated,' she said. 'The others were probably uninterested or not particularly inspired by Mozart or by the discussion.'

5 |

Dr Frances Rauscher, of the Centre for the Neurobiology of Learning and Memory in Berkeley, California, had suggested that students would do better after listening to Mozart because his music is complex and stimulates particular activity in the brain.

6 |

However, Dr Hallam did not dismiss the Californian idea, because the experiments were performed on adults, who may process music differently.

7 |

The Minister for Science said, 'If the results are conclusive, we could see a whole new approach in the future to the way pupils are taught in school.'

Answers and notes on page 65.

EXAM EXERCISE 2

You are going to read an article about making better use of time at work. Choose the most suitable heading from the list **A-H** for each part (**1-6**) of the article. There is one extra heading which you do not need to use. There is an example at the beginning (**0**).

A Inability to let others help
B Those in charge aware of problem
C Failure to take responsibility
D Employers and workers need to change
E Feeling there is too much to do
F Bad effects at home and at work
G Lacking a clear system
H Time spent working

MAKING BETTER USE OF TIME AT WORK

0 H

A recent survey by Austin Knight reveals that in British industry the 'long hours culture' is the new British disease. In their report of over 22 well-known British companies representing over one million workers, they found that British office workers have some of the longest hours in Europe, if not *the* longest.

1

They found that two out of three work 40 hours or more per week, 25 per cent work 50 hours or more. In addition, 76 per cent of these workers say that continually working long hours affects their physical health, 47 per cent say their families suffer and 45 per cent feel their work performance is undermined.

2

Oddly enough, 90 per cent of employers also see long hours as a problem because of reduced performance and lowered morale.

3

So, what can be done? Obviously one important step is that employers understand the potentially negative effects of long working hours on their employees' health, family and performance. However, there are strategies that individuals can engage in that will help them manage their time better.

4

There seem to be at least three different types of time wasters. First there is the 'mañana' type who feels that you should not 'do today what you can do tomorrow'. These are the procrastinators who see the job as 'too big' for them to handle. Some basic tips for these people are (1) to break up huge tasks into smaller jobs, (2) to draw up a list of things to do, with the most important tasks at the top and the least important at the bottom, (3) to balance routine tasks with more enjoyable ones and (4) to deal with each document that comes their way once only (read it, act upon it, file it or throw it away).

5

Second, there are the 'poor delegators', the people who feel that nobody can do a job as well as they can. They either want to retain the power or just feel it is part of the job, and feel that by not doing it, they are not fulfilling their responsibilities. The basic tips for these types are: (1) to accept that delegation does not mean giving up responsibility, (2) having delegated a job, to leave the person to get on with it, and (3) say 'no' politely to work that is outside their area of responsibility.

6

Finally, there is the disorganised type who is instantly recognised by piles of paper around his or her desk. These individuals miss or are late for appointments, forget or misplace papers and are frequently involved in trying to find lost telephone numbers, diary dates, and people's names. They need to do some of the following: (1) stick to one task and finish it, (2) buy a large note pad for writing down all notes, messages, etc., (3) clear the top of their desk and have only the task they are dealing with in front of them, (4) spend time setting up systems to gain control of the chaos.

Answers and notes on page 66.

EXAM EXERCISE 3

You are going to read an article about people falling in love on trains or at stations. Choose from the list **A-I** the sentence which best summarises each part (**1-7**) of the article. There is one extra sentence which you do not need to use. There is an example at the beginning (**0**).

A The romance was not ended by a problem early in the relationship.
B This man had a good reason for contacting the girl he had met.
C Taking a job overseas failed to end this relationship.
D A man feeling very tired got on a crowded train.
E A woman left her purse on the seat when she got off the train.
F This couple often travelled on the same train before they went out together.
G This man was not in a mood for talking to other people on the train.
H This couple met briefly when the man was changing trains at the station.
I One would not normally expect people to fall in love on trains or at stations.

RAILWAY ROMANCES

0	I

Noel Coward wrote a famous play in the 1950s called *Brief Encounter*. It tells of a couple who fell in love when they kept meeting in the waiting room of a railway station during wartime. For many people, a railway station or train must seem the most unromantic of places and yet there are plenty of examples of people meeting by chance on trains or at stations and falling in love.

1	

John was one such person who met his future wife as a result of falling asleep on a train. It was just before Christmas some years ago when John was travelling on a very early morning train back home to Liverpool to spend Christmas with his family. He had been out to a party the night before and was feeling very sleepy. The train was quite full but he managed to find an empty seat.

2	

"Liz, who is now my wife," says John, "jumped on the train just as it was pulling out of the station. She asked if the seat next to me was free and sat down. Normally I try to strike up a conversation with people on a train, but on this occasion I felt so tired that I just fell asleep. Some time later I woke up and realised, to my embarrassment, that I had been lying against her.

3	

"I felt that I could not ignore the woman now and began to chat. I discovered that, although she was going to Chester, she lived quite close to me and she gave me her phone number. After she had got off I found a purse on her seat. In the end it turned out that it did not belong to her but it gave me the perfect excuse for phoning her. You can guess the rest. We were married a few years later and now have got two little girls."

4	

Another person to find romance on the train was Ron, a keen football fan. Twenty years ago he was travelling to work every day on a train from Basingstoke to Southampton. He usually found himself sitting opposite a young woman called Mary. They would often talk to each other and then, after about five or six months, they decided to go out together one evening. Ron was to decide where to go but Mary told him to keep the destination a secret – they went to see a football match.

5	

"Mary had never been to a football match in her life," says Ron, "but our relationship took off from there. The problem came when I was offered a full-time job – as a football reporter – in Perth, Australia. Fortunately, Mary followed me, we got married and have been together now for over 21 years."

6	

A final example of a couple being brought together by the railways is Jimmy and Peggy. Jimmy was in the army during the Second World War and would sometimes have to wait for a connecting train at the station in Newcastle where Peggy lived. If he could let Peggy know that he would be on the station, she would come and meet him there and they would be able to spend a little time together.

7	

"Our romance nearly finished very early," says Jimmy. "On one of the first occasions we met, we walked out of the station and lost track of time. When we got back, the last train had gone and I had to take Peggy home. It was very late when we got there and her father was so angry that it seemed our friendship would be finished before it had really begun. Fortunately, Peggy managed to convince her father that I was not so bad and we went on to have many happy years together."

Answers and notes on page 66.

EXAM EXERCISE 4

You are going to read an article about a play. Choose the most suitable heading from the list **A-H** for each part (**1-6**) of the article. There is one extra heading which you do not need to use. There is an example at the beginning (**0**).

A Hidden emotion
B Change of setting
C Ashamed
D Permission granted
E Relief
F Tragedy
G Happier
H Unpromising start

A SAD ENDING BECOMES A HAPPY ENDING

0 H

In 1909 a play called *Liliom* was seen for the first time in Budapest. It had been written by Ferenc Molnár, a local man who had gained considerable success and fame from earlier plays. Unfortunately, this play was at first a failure and closed after only 26 performances. Ten years later, the play was revived and this time was an instant success and went on to be performed in a number of other countries.

1

The play was sombre. It told the story of a rough and unpleasant man, Liliom, who worked at a fairground. He fell in love with a local girl, whom he married even though he was never able to express his true feelings for her. Liliom treated his wife badly and eventually killed himself. Years later he was allowed to return to earth for one day to try to repair some of the wrong he had done, but he failed miserably.

2

The audiences in Budapest in 1909 were puzzled by the play's strange mixture of harsh realism and fantasy. Nevertheless, there was a clue to its meaning. Molnár was well-known in the city and people were aware that when he had written *Liliom,* his first marriage had been in difficulty. The couple had huge arguments and it was said that Molnár beat his wife. Molnár's plays often reflected his own life and it seemed likely that in the play he was trying to say that an unpleasant, even violent, exterior can hide a gentle nature. Molnár, like Liliom, had been unable to declare his love.

3

Despite the gloomy theme of the play, it was thought by several people that it could be set to music and made into an opera. Molnár refused to let this happen at first but then, in the early 1940s, he unexpectedly agreed to allow it to be made into an American musical. He had seen and enjoyed the musical *Oklahoma* by Richard Rodgers and Oscar Hammerstein and was happy to let them adapt his play.

4

To start with, Rodgers and Hammerstein were not keen on the idea but gradually they realised they could transfer the action from Budapest to a part of rural America at the end of the 19th century. The main character would also work in a fairground, fall in love, die and return to earth. The musical would be called *Carousel.*

5

The one major change which the writers wanted to make was to the ending, which they believed to be far too tragic for a musical. The change was made so that the show finished on a more positive note than *Liliom,* showing some hope for the future with the hero, Billy Bigelow, having had a little success in repairing some of the wrong he had done.

6

Richard Rodgers was very worried about how Molnár would react to having the ending of the play changed so drastically. Molnár came to watch the first full rehearsal. At the end Rodgers went nervously to him, certain that he would hate the new ending as it so completely altered the spirit of the original. He asked Molnár what he thought of the show. "What you have done," Molnár said, "is so beautiful. And you know what I like best? The ending."...

Answers and notes on page 66.

LOOKING AT PART 2

In this part of the test you have to read a passage which is followed by seven or eight questions. For each of the questions there are four suggested answers (A, B, C, D). Only one of these answers is correct; you must choose the answer which is correct and mark the appropriate letter on your answer sheet.

There is no example of a correct answer given in this part of the test.

Form of the questions

In most cases you will have a question followed by four possible answers. However, sometimes the question will take the form of a sentence which has not been finished. The four answers are then four different ways of ending the sentence, only one of which is correct.

Types of question asked

The questions in this part of the test are usually looking for a *detailed* understanding of parts of the passage which you have to read. However, some questions may ask you to show a more *general* understanding of parts of the passage or of the whole passage. The final question often asks you to show your general understanding of the passage.

The questions *usually* follow the same order as the passage, that is to say that the answer to question 2 will *usually* be found in the passage after the answer to question 1, and so on.

USE THE PASSAGE TO ANSWER THE QUESTIONS

You must always choose your answer according to what is written in the passage, even if you disagree with it. Sometimes you may see an answer that is totally untrue (e.g. *Paris is the capital of England*) but this does not necessarily mean that this is the wrong answer – for example, the question may be about something a person said in the passage even though what that person said was untrue. Remember, you are being asked to show your understanding of the passage, not to express your personal opinions or knowledge of a certain subject. If, for example, you had the sentence below in a passage along with the question following:

There is no doubt at all that all dogs are vicious.

Question: What are we told about dogs?

the answer would have to be that all dogs are vicious. It does not matter if you do not agree with the statement or if you know that it is untrue, you are being asked to show that you understand what has been written in the passage.

ANSWERING THE QUESTION ASKED

Be careful to answer the question asked. Quite often there is a statement in one of the answers which correctly refers to something in the passage but which does not answer the question asked. Such an answer would obviously be wrong. You might have the sentence below in a passage with the question which follows:

The old man was delighted with the present his daughter had given him.

Question: How do we know the daughter did not see her father every day?

One of the suggested answers could be: She had given him a present.

This is a true statement based on the passage but it does not answer the question asked.

Do not assume too much

Be careful not to think that a passage tells you more than it really does when choosing an answer. Look at the following sentence and question:

> At the end of his holiday Bob had hardly any money left.
> Question: What are we told about Bob at the end of his holiday?

One of the four suggested answers to this question could be: Bob had spent all his money.

This answer cannot be correct; if Bob had *hardly any money* left, this does mean he had a little left and that he had not spent quite everything. (If the answer was Bob had spent almost all his money, this would, of course, be correct.)

PRACTICE EXERCISES

Exercises 1-5

In the first five exercises, there are two questions on each passage with a choice of only three possible answers.

PRACTICE EXERCISE 1

A 20-year-old soldier was slightly injured last night when the car in which he was a passenger was in collision with a lorry on the main road between Cardiff and Swansea.

1 The soldier was
- **A** badly hurt.
- **B** hurt a little.
- **C** not hurt at all.

2 What do we know about the car?
- **A** It was travelling from Cardiff to Swansea.
- **B** It was being driven by a soldier.
- **C** It hit another vehicle on the road.

Now check your answers on page 67.

PRACTICE EXERCISE 2

Riches store will re-open for business next Monday following the fire which last month badly damaged the ground floor of the building. Repairs and improvements that have been carried out as a result of the fire should make shopping here an even more enjoyable experience than it was before.

1 As a result of the fire
- **A** the store had to close down for a time.
- **B** the ground floor was totally destroyed.
- **C** the store was able to open only on Mondays.

2 What should be the effect of the repairs?
- **A** More people are likely to shop here.
- **B** People will find them really enjoyable.
- **C** It should be pleasant to shop here.

Now check your answers on page 67.

PRACTICE EXERCISE 3

Three men were arrested at a flat in London last night in connection with a series of art thefts from large country houses in England and France. A fourth man, thought to be the leader of the gang, is still being sought by the police.

1 Why were the men arrested?
- **A** They were caught stealing a number of works of art.
- **B** It is thought they may have stolen some paintings.
- **C** They had broken into houses in many countries.

2 The fourth man
  A is still free.
  B is seeking the police.
  C wants to be the leader of the gang.

Now check your answers on page 67.

PRACTICE EXERCISE 4

In recent years, people in Britain have become increasingly conscious of the need to lead a more healthy life. As a result of this, food products containing a great deal of fat or sugar have become less popular and frequent exercise has become a way of life for many. By adopting a more healthy life style, people hope not only to live longer but also to feel fit and be active well into old age.

1 What evidence is there to show that people in Britain are trying to lead healthier lives?
  A Very few people eat food which has fat in it.
  B Many people take part in exercise.
  C People are aware of the need for a healthy life.

2 People are trying to lead a more healthy life
  A in order to become younger.
  B so that they can take exercise.
  C in order to remain active.

Now check your answers on page 67.

PRACTICE EXERCISE 5

The 10-mile race for pupils of Rickton School took place last Saturday. Fifty runners took part and all but two of them managed to complete the course. The race was won by 18-year-old Peter Sloane, who is in his final year at the school. Peter hopes to go to Hull University next year to study Physics, but is determined to find time whilst there to continue his running.

1 How many people finished the race?
  A 2 B 13 C 48

2 Peter Sloane
  A plans to run to the university.
  B intends to carry on studying next year.
  C has finished studying at school.

Now check your answers on page 67.

Exercises 6-10

In the remaining five exercises, there is a choice of four possible answers for each question (as in the examination). Exercises 6 and 7 have two questions each, exercises 8 and 9 have three questions, and exercise 10 has four questions.

PRACTICE EXERCISE 6

Flair Electronics have reported a drop in profits this year following disappointing sales figures for their new range of computer software. The Chairman of the company put the blame for this on the growth in the number of companies producing material of a similar nature.

1 Flair Electronics have .....
  A increased their losses this year.
  B made less money this year than last year.
  C increased their profits only slightly this year.
  D lost less money this year.

2 What do we know about the company's new range of computer software?
  A Many other companies produce computer software.
  B It does not work as well as had been expected.
  C It will be out of date by the end of the year.
  D The company has not sold as much of it as expected.

Now check your answers on page 67.

PRACTICE EXERCISE 7

The Lathkill Hotel is situated in the Derbyshire village of Over Haddon and enjoys spectacular panoramic views. The nearby tranquil dales and rolling fields are dotted with interesting villages, but there are larger towns too – Bakewell with its famous puddings, Buxton, the elegant spa town. Also nearby are five famous country houses (including Chatsworth), making the hotel an ideal base for exploring the area.

Home-cooked food is available at lunchtimes and evenings and you can eat while enjoying glorious views. During the summer you can take your pick from a hot and cold buffet table. Packed lunches are also available. A more extensive evening menu is available in the restaurant, which is open to residents and non-residents.

1 Why might people want to stay at this hotel?
- **A** There are no towns nearby.
- **B** The nearby countryside is very peaceful.
- **C** The hotel is lonely and isolated.
- **D** The country houses all welcome visitors.

2 The evening meals are different from the lunchtime meals because
- **A** there is more choice.
- **B** both hot and cold food is available.
- **C** non-residents may eat in the restaurant.
- **D** the restaurant is closed in summer.

Now check your answers on page 68.

PRACTICE EXERCISE 8

Every parent worries about what sort of world their children will inherit. As populations grow, clean safe water will become an even more vital commodity and so it is essential that children learn at an early age the importance of water and the environment we live in.

North West Water has built special educational facilities throughout the north west of England. These unique 'environmental classrooms' are available free of charge to any school in the region. Each facility provides a range of fun and interactive lessons where young people can learn how water reaches their homes and how they can help in conserving water.

Over 3,000 children a year spend time in the classrooms. It has been rated as a fantastic day out by both children and teachers. We think it is a responsible approach to education as we face up to the future.

1 According to the passage, what do parents worry about?
- **A** the amount of money they can leave to their children
- **B** how life will be for their children
- **C** the fact that there are more people in the world
- **D** whether the water children drink is clean

2 The special educational facilities
- **A** can be used free of charge by any school in England.
- **B** teach children how to take water home.
- **C** prevent children from wasting water.
- **D** allow children to learn in an enjoyable way.

3 Why does the writer think that North West Water has a responsible attitude to the future?
- **A** Because children are learning something important for the future.
- **B** Because the number of people in the world is falling.
- **C** Because so many children go to these special facilities.
- **D** Because children have a wonderful day out.

Now check your answers on page 68.

PRACTICE EXERCISE 9

Americans were invited to sample the food, the golf and the heritage of Scotland at a meeting held in New York yesterday to promote the tourism opportunities created by films set in Scotland. The move came as the Scottish Tourist Board announced a seven per cent growth in tourist spending in Scotland last year.

American tourism accounts for a quarter of the overseas visits to Scotland and visitor numbers are expected to increase substantially this year as a result of the large number of 'scenic' films shot there. At the Scottish Travel Fair in Glasgow, it was predicted that the films could have an effect on Scottish tourism for the next 15 years.

1 What was the reason for the meeting in New York?
- **A** to advertise films made in Scotland
- **B** to make Scottish food more popular
- **C** to encourage people to visit Scotland
- **D** to persuade people to make films in Scotland

2 Why might members of the Scottish Tourist Board be feeling pleased?
- **A** More tourists visited Scotland last year.
- **B** They had an increase in their salaries.
- **C** Visitors spent more money in Scotland last year.
- **D** They spent more money on visitors last year.

3 This year it is expected that
- **A** more people will come to visit Scotland.
- **B** there will be an increase in 'scenic' films made here.
- **C** the films will have little effect on the number of visitors.
- **D** a quarter of all visitors will come from America.

Now check your answers on page 68.

PRACTICE EXERCISE 10

A 35-year old man from Leeds walked into his hotel in Keswick in the English Lake District at eight o'clock last night as the local mountain rescue team were preparing to mount a search for him. The man, an inexperienced mountain walker, had had an argument with his wife that morning and had left the hotel to go walking despite warnings of severe weather conditions. He had been reported missing by his wife late in the afternoon.

In fact the man had not been in the mountains at all but, on seeing how bad the weather was, had changed his mind and had decided to take a bus to Windermere. He did not think to phone his wife to tell her of his change of plans. Unfortunately, he missed the bus which he had planned to catch back to Keswick and arrived at the hotel rather later than he had intended.

1 Why was the mountain rescue team going to search for the man?
- **A** It was thought that he was lost in the mountains.
- **B** The man was not an experienced mountaineer.
- **C** The weather was not going to improve.
- **D** The man had left the hotel in a bad temper.

2 What do we know about the man?
- **A** He was not used to walking in the mountains.
- **B** He had many arguments with his wife.
- **C** He did not know about the bad weather.
- **D** He had thought of phoning his wife.

3 Why do you think the man's wife was worried about him?
- **A** He had changed his plans.
- **B** He had gone to Windermere.
- **C** He had missed a bus.
- **D** He had not returned to the hotel.

4 Why did the man arrive back at the hotel later than he had intended?
  A The bus was held up by the bad weather.
  B He did not catch the bus he wanted.
  C He missed the bus to Windermere.
  D The bus left Windermere early.

Now check your answers on page 68.

DOING THE EXAM

1 First of all, read through the questions in order to get an idea of what the passage is about.

2 Then read through the whole passage but do *not* begin to choose answers to the questions.

3 Read through the first question and try to find the answer in the passage.

4 Now read through the choice of possible answers and try to decide which one is correct; mark the appropriate letter on your answer sheet.

5 If you cannot decide which answer is correct, move on to the next question and follow the instructions in numbers 3 and 4 above.

6 When you have answered all the questions you can, go back to those questions which you have not answered and try again to decide which is the correct answer.

Remember

- Only one answer for each question will be correct. *Never* mark more than one letter for one answer.
- Do not choose an answer simply because it has in it an unusual word which is also found in a part of the passage that the question refers to. This may possibly be a catch. The answer *may* be the correct one or it *may not* be. Read the question, the appropriate part of the passage and all the suggested answers carefully before choosing your answer.
- Do not choose an answer simply because you agree with what it says. Always use the passage to choose your answer – the person writing it may have a different opinion from you.
- Read each question carefully and make sure that the answer you choose actually answers the question which is being asked.
- If you miss out an answer, make sure that when you put in the next answer, you put it by the correct number (that is to say that if, for example, you missed out answer 8, do not put answer 9 at the side of number 8).
- If you change your mind about an answer, remember to rub out the answer you had already indicated.
- Always mark one of the letters on the answer sheet even if, after thinking about the item, you are simply guessing the answer. There is always a chance that you may be right.

EXAM EXERCISES

EXAM EXERCISE 1

You are going to read an article about soap operas. For the questions which follow, choose the answer (**A**, **B**, **C**, or **D**) which you think fits best according to the text.

In the 1930s, when radio was still in its infancy, broadcasting stations in the USA wondered what type of programmes they should put on during the daytime. They came up with the idea of producing serials that would be on the radio every afternoon telling a continuous story. To keep the listeners' interest, there would be far more crises occurring than in real life. Knowing that the majority of the audience would be women, the broadcasters decided that the women in the serials would be strong characters and the men weak. The serials were an instant success with listeners. As the radio stations were paid for by advertising, these programmes always carried advertisements and, since one of the most frequently advertised products was soap, the programmes became known as *Soaps* or *Soap Operas*.

It was really by chance that the soap opera appeared in Britain. The BBC (British Broadcasting Corporation) had no interest in producing this type of programme but during the Second World War it was thought that the Americans should be shown how well the British people were standing up to the war. For this reason, a soap opera was written for the North American service of the BBC; it was called *Front Line Family* and showed how a typical English family, the Robinsons, were living during the war. Some people in Britain managed to hear the programme and asked for it to be broadcast for the British audience. The BBC were unwilling to do this but finally agreed and broadcast the programme in Britain, but changed the name to *The Robinsons*. The programme ran for six years.

Other soaps were introduced later, one telling the life of a doctor's family and another, *The Archers*, about life in a country village. The original aim of *The Archers* was to inform farmers of new developments in agriculture. The serial began in 1951 and is still to be heard on five evenings every week.

Some attempts at soap opera began to appear on television in Britain in the mid-1950s but it was not until 1961 that the first *real* soap opera appeared. This was shown, not by the BBC, but by commercial television. The serial, called *Coronation Street,* was about the lives of people living in a working-class street near Manchester. Although the serial was planned to run for only thirteen weeks, it is still to be seen several nights every week and almost every week has more viewers than any other programme on British television.

The BBC never managed to produce a really successful soap opera until 1984, when it introduced *Eastenders*. This programme is about life in an area of the east end of London. For a time it had more viewers than *Coronation Street* and still rivals it as the most popular programme on British television. There is a major difference between the two programmes in that *Eastenders* concentrates on often rather depressing realism whilst *Coronation Street*, although having serious storylines, always contains a strong element of comedy.

1 What problem did broadcasting stations in America have in the early days of radio?
- **A** how to reflect real life
- **B** what to broadcast during the day
- **C** what type of serial to produce
- **D** how to entertain women

2 Why did the radio stations make women have the strongest characters in soap operas?
- **A** Because men usually have weak characters.
- **B** Because no men would be listening.
- **C** Because women deal better with crises.
- **D** Because the audience would be mainly female.

3 Why was the name *soap* or *soap opera* given to these programmes?
- **A** Soap was often advertised during the programmes.
- **B** Soap companies advertised the programmes.
- **C** Soap companies owned several radio stations.
- **D** Soap was the only product advertised during the programmes.

4 Why was the programme *Front Line Family* made?
- **A** to tell the Americans why the British were at war
- **B** to tell the Americans how the British were living during the war
- **C** to tell the Americans how the British were winning the war
- **D** to tell the Americans why the British stood to win the war

5 Why did the BBC begin to broadcast *Front Line Family* in Britain?
- **A** Because people in America liked it.
- **B** Because the BBC thought it would run for six years.
- **C** Because people asked to hear it.
- **D** Because the BBC changed its name.

6 What do we learn about *The Archers* in this passage?
- **A** The programme was about a country doctor.
- **B** It could be heard every evening of the week.
- **C** It was first broadcast before 1951.
- **D** The aim of the programme was to educate farmers.

7 What do we learn about *Coronation Street?*
- **A** It has always been the most popular programme on television.
- **B** It has lasted longer than expected.
- **C** It was the first real soap on to be shown on BBC television.
- **D** It takes place in central Manchester.

8 How is *Coronation Street* different from *Eastenders?*
- **A** It is funnier.
- **B** It has a stronger storyline.
- **C** It is more serious.
- **D** It is more like real life.

Answers and notes on page 69.

EXAM EXERCISE 2

You are going to read an article about early aeroplane flights. For the questions which follow, choose the answer (**A**, **B**, **C**, or **D**) which you think fits best according to the text.

For five years from December 1903 to September 1908, two young bicycle mechanics from the state of Ohio in America repeatedly claimed that they had built a heavier-than-air machine which they had flown successfully. Despite demonstrations and photographs of themselves flying, the claims of Wilbur and Orville Wright were laughed at and dismissed as a practical joke by the magazine *Scientific American*, the newspaper the *New York Herald*, the US Army and most American scientists.

Experts rejected the Wright brothers' claim without troubling to examine the evidence as they were so convinced, on purely scientific grounds, that flight in powered machines which were heavier than air was impossible. It was not until President Theodore Roosevelt ordered public trials at Fort Myers in 1908 that the Wrights were able to prove their claim conclusively and the Army and the scientific press were compelled to accept that their flying machine was a reality.

It is perhaps not too surprising that a couple of young bicycle mechanics in a remote town on the prairies should be ignored by the intellectuals of the more sophisticated east coast of America at a time when the horse was still the principal means of transport. What is more surprising is that the local newspapers in their home town of Dayton, Ohio, should have ignored the Wrights. In 1904, a local banker, Torrence Huffman, allowed the brothers to use a large piece of farm land owned by him outside the town for their flying experiments. The land was bordered by two main roads and the local railway line so that, as the months went by, hundreds of people actually saw the Wrights flying.

Many of the amazed passengers wrote to the local newspapers to ask who were the young men who were regularly flying near the railway line and why had nothing appeared about them in the papers. Eventually the enquiries became so frequent that the papers complained that they were becoming a nuisance, but still their editors showed no interest in the story, sending neither a reporter nor a photographer.

In 1940, Dan Kumler, the city editor of the Dayton *Daily News* at the time of the flights gave an interview about his refusal to publish anything thirty-five years earlier and spoke frankly about his reasons. Kumler recalled, "I guess we just didn't believe it. Of course, you must remember that the Wrights at that time kept things very secret."

The interviewer responded in amazement, "You mean they kept things secret by flying over an open field?" Kumler considered the question, grinned and said, "I guess the truth is we were just plain stupid."

1 What do we learn about the Wright brothers in the first paragraph?
- **A** They said they had built a flying machine.
- **B** They gave lots of flying demonstrations.
- **C** They laughed at the ideas in the *Scientific American*.
- **D** They took photographs of themselves.

2 How did Theodore Roosevelt become involved with the Wright brothers?
- **A** He insisted that the trial should be in a public court.
- **B** He concluded that the brothers were telling the truth.
- **C** He ordered the press to tell the truth about the plane.
- **D** He ordered the brothers to test the plane in public.

3 Why are horses mentioned in the third paragraph?
- **A** They were used only in the East.
- **B** They provided the usual way of travelling.
- **C** They were rarely used in Ohio.
- **D** They were the only form of transport.

4 What does the writer find surprising about the flying experiments?
- **A** the lack of interest shown by local newspapers
- **B** the attitude of the experts
- **C** the lack of flying experiments in the East
- **D** the skill of bicycle mechanics

5 Torrence Huffman helped the Wright brothers by
- **A** lending them money to buy some land.
- **B** letting them use some of his land.
- **C** giving them some of his farm land.
- **D** allowing them to buy some land.

6 Why did people write to the newspapers?
- **A** to ask why people were flying near the railway line
- **B** to make sure that it was the Wright brothers who were flying
- **C** to ask why the flights had not been reported in the papers
- **D** to complain about the nuisance caused by these flights

7 Why was the interviewer surprised by the first answer given by Dan Kumler?
- **A** The interviewer knew that the Wrights had opened the gates to the field.
- **B** The interviewer thought the Wrights had wanted to keep their flights secret.
- **C** The interviewer did not believe what Kumler had told the Wrights.
- **D** The interviewer thought that anybody could have seen the Wrights flying.

8 Which of the following would be a suitable title?
- **A** Newspapers tell lies
- **B** Too easily convinced
- **C** Refusal to recognise progress
- **D** People will believe anything

Answers and notes on page 69.

EXAM EXERCISE 3

You are going to read an article about the Carnegie Hall in New York. For the questions which follow, choose the answer (**A**, **B**, **C**, or **D**) which you think fits best according to the text.

One of the most famous concert halls in America is the Carnegie Hall in New York. Initially, it was called simply the 'Music Hall', but three years after its opening it was renamed in honour of Andrew Carnegie, the man who had provided much of the finance for its building.

The Hall officially opened on May 5, 1891. Since then the Hall has played host to the giants of classical music, as well as those of jazz, pop, folk and rock music, and has also been used for political rallies, religious services and lectures.

One of the most dramatic lectures given in the Hall took place during its first year. This began simply as a talk accompanied by slides of paintings of sunsets and landscapes, which was what the audience had been expecting. However, as the lecture progressed, the effects became more dramatic, with thunder, rolling clouds and steam billowing over the audience's head while mechanical volcanoes exploded on stage – all to the amazement and delight of the audience.

In 1927 the violinist Yehudi Menuhin made his appearance at the Carnegie Hall for the first time – he was aged ten. In the afternoon before the performance, he was wandering around the Hall instead of practising and was fascinated by an axe which he saw on the wall. The axe was for use in a fire but the boy, not knowing this, asked a security guard what it was for. The guard made an impression with his reply: "That's for chopping the heads off soloists who don't play well enough. Quite a few have already been chopped off." Yehudi went rushing back to practise.

On one occasion another famous violinist and a pianist were giving a performance together when the violinist got lost in the music. He anxiously looked to the pianist for help and whispered "Where are we?". He received the less than helpful reply "In the Carnegie Hall".

Rock and roll made its first appearance at the Carnegie Hall in 1955 with Bill Haley and his Comets. In 1964 the British invasion arrived when the Beatles played their first concert here. On the day of the concert, cars came to a halt all over the city and the crowds surrounding the building were enormous. Fortunately, in all the chaos nobody was seriously injured and the Hall escaped with only minor damage.

In the 1950s the building was threatened with demolition but a vigorous campaign to save it was led by the conductor, Isaac Stern. In 1960 the Hall was purchased by the City of New York and a few years later it was named a national landmark. Over the years the most famous musicians, singers and entertainers in the world have appeared there – no doubt they will continue to do so for many years to come.

1 What do we learn about Andrew Carnegie?
- **A** He gave most of his money to the Hall.
- **B** He renamed the Hall.
- **C** He gave money to help build the Hall .
- **D** He felt honoured when the name was changed.

2 Why was the audience surprised at the lecture in the first year?
- **A** People thought that the special effects were frightening.
- **B** People had not been expecting to see slides.
- **C** People had expected the lecture to be rather more dramatic.
- **D** People had thought they were going to hear a straightforward lecture.

3 What would seem to be special about Yehudi Menuhin's appearance at the Hall in 1927?
- **A** He did no practising for the concert at all.
- **B** He was very young at the time.
- **C** He had played here before.
- **D** He had not appeared on a stage before.

4 Why do you imagine he went to practise after speaking to the security guard?
- **A** He realised that he needed to practise.
- **B** He believed what the guard had told him.
- **C** He thought the guard would attack him.
- **D** He wanted to find out what the axe was for.

5 Why was the pianist's answer unhelpful?
- **A** The violinist knew he was in the Carnegie Hall.
- **B** The pianist was not telling the truth.
- **C** The violinist had lost his music.
- **D** The pianist did not know where they were.

6 What happened as a result of the Beatles going to Carnegie Hall?
- **A** A few people were seriously injured.
- **B** There were crowds in all parts of New York.
- **C** Some people escaped from the Hall uninjured.
- **D** There were traffic jams in New York.

7 What happened in the 1950s?
- **A** Isaac Stern stopped the demolition of the Hall.
- **B** The Hall was sold to the City of New York.
- **C** There was a possibility of the Hall being pulled down.
- **D** There was a campaign to demolish the Hall.

8 What does the writer seem to think about the future of the Carnegie Hall.
- **A** The greatest entertainers in the world have appeared there.
- **B** No one can tell what the future will bring.
- **C** It will become a national landmark.
- **D** It will continue to attract great stars.

Answers and notes on page 70.

EXAM EXERCISE 4

You are going to read an article about a man's memories from his childhood. For the questions which follow, choose the answer (**A**, **B**, **C**, or **D**) which you think fits best according to the text.

Father was in the army all through the war – the First War, I mean – so, up to the age of five, I never saw much of him, and what I saw did not worry me. Sometimes I woke and there was a big figure looking down at me. Sometimes in the early morning I heard the closing of the front door and the sound of boots walking down the lane. These were Father's entrances and exits.

In fact, I rather liked his visits, though it was an uncomfortable squeeze between Mother and him when I got into the big bed in the early morning. He smoked, which gave him a pleasant sort of smell. Watching him shave was fascinating. Each time he went away, he left lots of souvenirs – model tanks, knives, cap badges and all sorts of military equipment which he put in a long box on top of the wardrobe as he felt that they could be handy sometime. When he was not there, Mother let me get a chair and search through his treasures. She did not seem to think so highly of them as he did.

The war was the most peaceful period of my life. Every morning I awoke as soon as it was light and felt myself to be like the sun, ready to shine and rejoice. Life never seemed so simple and clear and full of possibilities as then. I got up, went into Mother's room and climbed into the big bed. She woke and I began to tell her of my schemes. I talked but then fell asleep and woke again only when I heard her below in the kitchen, making the breakfast.

I often wondered what Mother and I should do all day, what present I would get for Christmas and what I should do to brighten up the home. There was that little matter of the baby, for instance. Mother and I could never agree about that. Ours was the only house in the street without a new baby, and Mother said we could not afford one until Father came back from the war as they were very expensive. That showed how simple she was. The Geneys who lived nearby had a baby, and everybody knew that they had hardly any money at all. Admittedly it was probably a cheap baby, and Mother wanted something really good, but I felt this did not really matter. The Geney's baby would have been fine for us.

1 Until the age of five, the writer
- **A** did not worry his father.
- **B** never saw his father.
- **C** often annoyed his father.
- **D** saw his father occasionally.

2 Why did he find it uncomfortable being in the big bed when his father was home?
- **A** His mother squeezed him.
- **B** The bed did not have enough room for three.
- **C** He was not used to being in it so early.
- **D** His father smelt of smoke.

3 The writer's father kept his souvenirs because he thought
- **A** they could be put inside the wardrobe.
- **B** they were very valuable.
- **C** Mother did not seem to value them.
- **D** they might be useful.

4 When the writer woke up, he felt that
- **A** life was good.
- **B** he was simple.
- **C** life was possible.
- **D** he was funny.

5 What happened as soon as the writer got into his mother's bed?
- **A** She went to make breakfast.
- **B** He told her all his plans.
- **C** She asked him about his schemes.
- **D** He went to sleep.

6 The writer's mother said they could not have a baby because
- **A** there was a war on.
- **B** there were too many babies in the street.
- **C** they cost a lot of money.
- **D** Father was not at home.

7 Why did the writer think that his mother would not have wanted the Geney's baby?
- **A** It was probably not of very good quality.
- **B** The price would have been too high.
- **C** The Geneys were too poor.
- **D** She probably thought it was too good for her.

Answers and notes on page 71.

LOOKING AT PART 3

In this part of the test you have a passage which has a number of gaps in it. These gaps are where sentences or whole paragraphs are missing. After the passage there is a list of these missing sentences or paragraphs in a mixed up order. You have to decide which sentence or paragraph fills each gap best.

There is a letter in front of each sentence or paragraph; you must mark this letter on your answer sheet when you have found which gap the sentence or paragraph fills. The first gap (which always has the number 0) is an example and is done for you. There will always be one sentence or paragraph spare which does not fill any of the gaps.

Sometimes the passage will consist of a number of missing sentences, at other times it will consist of a number of missing paragraphs. The passage will never consist of a mixture of missing sentences and paragraphs.

CHOOSING THE RIGHT ANSWER

In order to put each sentence (or paragraph) in the correct place, you must get a good understanding of both the paragraphs and the sentences and decide which ones are closely connected.

When you are trying to decide in which paragraph a sentence should be placed, you will obviously look at the sentence in front of the gap. However, it is just as important to look at the sentence after the gap as sometimes you will find that a suggested answer fits quite well with the sentence that goes before it but does not fit in with the sentence which follows. Look at this example of a short paragraph followed by a choice of two sentences to put in the gap:

John was a young man who had spent all his life in the city and knew little about the countryside. (1) .... John found the work really hard but at the end said that he had really enjoyed himself.

A In order to get some idea of life in the country, he went for a holiday at a hotel in a tiny village.

B In order to get some idea of life in the country, he arranged to spend a few weeks working on a farm.

Sentence A fits in quite well with the first sentence of the paragraph – by staying at a hotel in a tiny village he would be able to learn something about the countryside. However, there is no suggestion that he did any work when he was there; this clearly does not fit in with the idea of the work being hard, as mentioned in the final sentence of the paragraph. However, sentence B fits in with both the first and last sentence – the mention of John working in B is connected with his finding work hard in the final sentence.

KEY WORDS

Although you will need to read the paragraphs and sentences for their meaning, you will often find key words which link a sentence to the subject of one of the paragraphs. When you look at the notes in the answers to the exercises below, you will see reference made to some of these words which link paragraphs and sentences.

Words such as *this*, *that*, *these*, *those* often link different parts of a paragraph. Similarly a person who has just been mentioned by his or her full name will then be referred to as *he* or *she* (or simply by his or her first or last name). Nouns when they first appear in a passage often have the word *a* in front of them; when they appear again, they usually have *the* in front of them.

PRACTICE EXERCISES

Exercises 1-4

In the first four exercises there are several sentences, each of which has a letter in front of it. The sentences are in the wrong order. You must work out the correct order so that the sentences read like a short newspaper article. Write down the appropriate letters in the correct order.

PRACTICE EXERCISE 1

A Police are warning members of the public to make sure all windows are closed.
B The thieves entered the house by means of an open window on the ground floor.
C It is the fifth time in nine days that thieves have entered houses in this way in Bedworth.
D A large amount of jewellery was stolen from a house in Bedworth last night.

Now check your answer on page 72.

PRACTICE EXERCISE 2

A The horse ran wildly down the road, causing several cars to have to stop suddenly.
B A dangerous situation developed on a road near Newbury last week.
C The owner of the horse pursued the animal in his car and after ten minutes managed to overtake it and stop it.
D A horse which was being put into a horse box to take it to a race meeting broke free from its handlers.

Now check your answer on page 72.

PRACTICE EXERCISE 3

A Several other companies are now considering similar campaigns.
B There has been a marked increase in the sales of Rileys biscuits.
C The campaign has taken the form of a series of advertisements which tell a continuing story.
D This has been attributed to a new television advertising campaign which began two months ago.
E Peter James, the director of the campaign, says that people take a greater interest in the advertisements as they want to know what happens next in the story.

Now check your answer on page 72.

PRACTICE EXERCISE 4

A Jane's story was about the effect that meeting a famous singer had on a small girl.
B As yet she has no ideas as to what to do with the money.
C Jane admits that much of the story is based on an incident in her own life.
D Jane Aston has won first prize for a short story which she wrote in a competition organised by a national newspaper.
E The prize of £5,000 will be presented to Jane in London later this month.

Now check your answer on page 72.

Exercises 5-8

In the next four exercises a sentence has been removed from the passage. Choose from the four suggested sentences **A**, **B**, **C**, **D**, which best fills the gap.

PRACTICE EXERCISE 5

A chaotic situation developed yesterday when traffic lights failed to work at a busy junction near Leeds. (5) .... Although police were on the scene within ten minutes, a queue over four kilometres long had already built up.

A Fortunately, only two or three vehicles were on the road at the time.
B The morning rush hour had just begun when lights on the road to Leeds became stuck on red.
C Fortunately, a passing policeman was immediately able to bring the situation under control.
D The problem became worse when the lights stopped working.

Now check your answer on page 72.

PRACTICE EXERCISE 6

Shoppers in Weatherfield will be pleased to learn that Bettabuys supermarket will in future open earlier and close later. Opening hours on every day apart from Sunday will be from 8.30 a.m. until 8.00 p.m. (6) .... "It has become obvious," said Mr Williams, "that many people like to shop either before or after work."

A Paul Williams, the supermarket manager, said the staff were already working long enough.
B Paul Williams, the supermarket manager, said that customers had found the old opening hours quite satisfactory.
C Paul Williams, the supermarket manager, said the store was responding to customer demand.
D Paul Williams, the supermarket manager, said that few people wanted to shop after working all day.

Now check your answer on page 72.

PRACTICE EXERCISE 7

The old sweet factory on Bristol Road is to be demolished in the next few weeks. (7) .... It is thought that the land has been bought by a local developer who has plans to build a block of luxury flats there.

A The factory closed down over eight years ago and has become an easy target for vandals.
B The factory was pulled down shortly after the demolition was announced.
C The factory has been empty for several years but is due to re-open in a few weeks' time.
D The factory will not be pulled down if a buyer for the land can be found.

Now check your answer on page 72.

PRACTICE EXERCISE 8

A postman was knocked down whilst delivering letters on Lancaster Avenue last Tuesday. Luckily, a nurse happened to be passing at the time and was able to administer first aid on the spot. (8) .... He is making good progress and should be able to return home within the next few days.

A The postman was not seriously injured and was able to continue delivering letters.
B A young man phoned for an ambulance, which arrived on the scene very quickly.
C An ambulance arrived but it was decided not to take the man to hospital.
D The postman was taken to hospital with injuries to his back and left leg.

Now check your answer on page 73.

Exercise 9

In the final exercise there are several gaps in the passage followed by a choice of sentences, **A**, **B**, **C**, **D**, to fill the gaps. There is a spare sentence that cannot fill any of the gaps.

PRACTICE EXERCISE 9

Lees Primary School will be a different place in future, following the retirement from teaching of Mrs Joan Wilson. (1) .... She received a mass of presents from pupils, former pupils, parents and members of staff on the last day of term.

Mrs Wilson told us that there have been tremendous changes in schools since she began teaching. (2) .... Possibly the most noticeable change has been in computers; when she began teaching these had hardly been heard of but now the school has a room full of them.

Mrs Wilson told us that although she would miss the children, she was looking forward to taking things easy in retirement. (3) .... Apart from this, though, she has as yet no special plans for the future.

A She is glad to say that in her opinion most of them have been for the good.
B She began her new job teaching at a school in central London several weeks ago.
C She plans to leave shortly for Australia, where she will spend three months with her sister.
D Mrs Wilson first began teaching at the school 36 years ago and for the last 25 years has been headmistress.

Now check your answers on page 73.

DOING THE EXAM

1 Read through the passage fairly quickly to get an idea of what it is about.
2 Now read through the list of missing sentences or paragraphs.
3 Read through the first paragraph and note the answer given for the example. Cross out the example on the list.
4 Now read the next paragraph as far as the first gap and then look through the list of suggested sentences and paragraphs. If you think you know the answer, mark the appropriate letter on the answer sheet and *lightly* cross out the answer on the question paper.
5 If you cannot decide on the correct answer, go on to the next part of the passage until you come to the next gap. Repeat what is suggested in number 4 above.
6 When you come to the end of the passage, go back and try to find the answer for any gaps which you have missed.
7 Always cross out an answer lightly when you have found it. Do this so that you do not keep looking at it every time you are looking for a new answer. However, your crossing out should always be light so that you can still read this answer in case you change your mind.

Remember

- Only one of the sentences or paragraphs will be suitable for each gap. *Never* mark more than one letter for one answer.
- One of the phrases will not be suitable for any gap, so that when you come to the end of this part of the paper, there will still be one phrase which you have not used.
- Read the words which follow a gap as well as those in front of it when choosing an answer.
- If you miss out an answer, make sure that when you put in the next answer, you put it by the correct number (that is to say that if, for example, you missed out answer 17, do not put answer 18 at the side of number 17).
- If you change your mind about an answer, remember to rub out the answer you had already indicated.
- Be careful not to mark the answer for the example as your first answer.
- Always mark one of the letters on the answer sheet even if, after thinking about the item, you are simply guessing the answer. There is always a chance that you may be right.

EXAM EXERCISES

EXAM EXERCISE 1

Read the following passage and then choose from the sentences **A-I** which one best fits each gap. There is one extra sentence which you will not need to use.

QANTAS

The Australian airline Qantas was founded in 1920. Queensland and Northern Territories Aerial Services, from which the word Qantas derives, is the longest-serving airline in the English-speaking world and the second longest-serving airline world-wide.

0	E

The airline was formed by two former Australian Flying Corps officers, W.Hudson Fysh and P.J.McGuniness. They were keen to enter a contest with a prize of £10,000 for the first Australian to fly from England to Australia in less than 28 days. Unfortunately, they were prevented from entering the race by the death of the man who had offered to provide money to pay their expenses.

1	

It took Fysh and McGuiness fifty-one days to plan the route, travelling by car through the thinly populated territory on poorly built roads that were often flooded in the wet season.

2 ____________

After a chance meeting with Fergus McMaster, a wealthy cattle farmer who agreed to give the two financial support, Fysh and McGuiness were on their way to making their dream of connecting far-distant parts of the continent by air a reality.

3 ____________

On November 2, 1922, a larger plane was bought by Qantas and the airline's first regular mail and passenger flights began between Charleville and Cloncurry. Qantas' services grew throughout the 1920s. An important landmark along the way came in March 1928 when Qantas was contracted to operate the first flying doctor service to sick people in remote parts of the country.

4 ____________

In 1934 the airline changed its name to Qantas Empire Airways Ltd, reflecting its desire to expand beyond the borders of Australia. Air mail services first to Singapore and soon after to Britain began in 1935.

5 ____________

In 1947 Qantas became a national airline when the government purchased the company. In December of that year the airline's first passenger service between Sydney and London was introduced.

6 ____________

Important changes in the airline industry announced in 1992 meant that aviation reforms would result in Qantas and Australian, the airline which links cities within Australia, becoming one.

7 ____________

A In the following years more overseas passenger services were introduced linking Australia with countries all over the world – Japan, Hong Kong, South Africa, the United States.

B Australian were at first in favour of joining Qantas but eventually decided to remain independent.

C However, they were asked by the government to plan a route and landing sites across the Northern Territory and Western Australia that would be used for the race.

D The service flew 255 patients more than 30,000 kilometres in its first year.

E Although it is now well-respected as an international carrier which flies people around the world in style, the airline's origins were rather more humble.

F Qantas bought Australian and agreed to the new name: Qantas, The Australian Airline.

G It was in the same year that the airline carried its first overseas passenger on a flight from Brisbane to Singapore.

H In 1920 they bought their first plane and then a second one soon after and for the first two years of Qantas' life, the planes were used as an air taxi service and for pleasure flights.

I Their experience on the journey convinced them that air travel was a necessity in such a huge country with often inhospitable terrain.

Answers and notes on page 73.

EXAM EXERCISE 2

Read the following passage and then choose from the sentences **A-H** which one best fits each gap. There is one extra sentence which you will not need to use.

POLICE TO USE BUSES

Police officers in one part of England are exchanging their cars for the bus, to cut down on expense and to improve efficiency. **0** G

Most of the buses are double deckers and police officers will be encouraged to sit on the top deck. **1** ______

Officers have been issued with timetables so that they can avoid long waits at bus stops. A police inspector said he did not want them waiting around thirty to forty minutes for a bus as this would clearly be a waste of police time. **2** ______ "If a bus is full, we will have to stand or wait for another one," he said.

Officers in uniform, detectives and traffic wardens will all use buses during a six month trial of the scheme. **3** ______ However, buses would be used when officers are involved in non-urgent routine business such as going to take statements or when returning from court appointments.

Senior police officers believe that the scheme will be effective in cutting down crime on public transport and will lead to a reduction in spending by the police force. **4** ______

A policewoman said: "I am all in favour of the idea. **5** ______ If it's good enough for them, it's good enough for us."

The transport manager for the local bus company which is sponsoring the scheme said: "This scheme will help the police and give peace of mind to the travelling public. **6** ______ We are hoping that the scheme will become permanent."

A It is thought that if they sit here, this will help to discourage crime as they will be able to see and to be seen clearly.
B The scheme will make life safer not only for passengers but also for our bus drivers.
C Obviously buses will not be used when officers are responding to emergency calls.
D We have always found the scheme very successful in the past.
E However, he did not expect the police to be treated differently from the rest of the public.
F It is good for the public, who will be able to see us and talk to us on the buses.
G They are to be allowed to travel free on buses in Northampton upon production of their identity card.
H Having police officers travel free on buses is cheaper than sending patrol cars to pick them up in order to return them to the police station.

Answers and notes on page 74.

EXAM EXERCISE 3

Read the following passage and then choose from the sentences **A-I** which one best fits each gap. There is one extra sentence which you will not need to use.

LOOKING FOR WORK

I was delighted when I finally left school at the end of October 1927. Now at last I felt I was a man. **0** B

Every day there were long queues at the Labour Exchange of people looking for work. Those of us who had just left school had to go to the Labour Exchange for an interview with a group of officials, employers and teachers. There we were asked questions about our ambitions, how suitable we were for certain types of work and how well we had done at school. **1** ______

After this we were required to attend the Youth Employment Department every day to see if any suitable jobs had been found. If it happened that a firm was in need of a youth, then a number of us would be given a green card which we were to take to the interview. **2** ______

I lost count of how many of these cards I received without finding a job. **3** ______ Twelve months passed and I still had found nothing.

On one occasion, my search had the surprising result of providing a very good job for one of my uncles. This uncle, who had been out of work for almost a year, was in his early thirties. **4** ______ My uncle kindly offered to take me to the firm as I did not know where it was.

When we arrived at the firm, the manager told us that he had found someone for the job just ten minutes earlier. However, looking at my uncle, he said: "We are looking for someone to operate a special machine, someone older than this boy. Are you interested?" My uncle accepted immediately. **5** ______

Eventually I was lucky, and just because two people had the same name. In town there was a tailor's called Brownson's and almost opposite was a cleaner's called Smith and Sons. Somewhat confusingly, the manageress of Smith and Sons was also called Brownson. **6** ______

The boy left and the clerk was filling in a card for me to go to the same place. The manager had heard what the clerk had said and came and told her that it was not Mr Brownson who needed an assistant but Miss Brownson of Smith and Sons. **7** ______ I am ashamed to say that I did not tell the boy any such thing – but I did get the job.

- **A** One day he heard that there was a vacancy for a young boy at a machine builders in Ashton-under-Lyne.
- **B** I was sure I would soon find myself a job and have money to spend.
- **C** In fact he had worked for only six months immediately after leaving school.
- **D** To prove that we had attended, the employer would sign the card.
- **E** The clerk asked me to run after the other boy to correct the mistake and make sure he went to the right shop.
- **F** We also looked through the newspapers, of course, hoping to find something in the job advertisements.
- **G** On the day in question, the clerk at the Youth Employment Department gave the boy in front of me in the queue a green card and told him to go to Mr Brownson's as he needed an assistant.
- **H** Our answers to these questions were then compared with a list of vacancies existing in the district.
- **I** He worked there until he retired at the age of sixty-five.

Answers and notes on page 74.

EXAM EXERCISE 4

Read the following passage and then choose from the paragraphs **A-H** which one best fits each gap. There is one extra paragraph which you will not need to use.

HORSE RACING

One of the most popular spectator sports in England is horse racing. There are race courses in all parts of the country and on most days of the year there will be two or three race meetings taking place.

0	D

There are basically two types of horse racing – jump racing and flat racing. As the names suggest, in jump racing the horses have to jump over fences whilst in flat racing they simply have to run as fast as possible along a flat track.

1	

It might be thought that jump racing would be considered the more important type of racing as horses not only have to run but also have to jump. In fact, the reverse is true, as flat racing is considered to be superior.

2	

Unfortunately, but inevitably, racing is a dangerous sport for the jockeys who ride the horses. Jockeys in jump races risk injuries not only from hitting the ground if they fall off their horse but also from being hit by other horses if they fall at a fence.

3	

Jockeys love to ride but, as most of them do not earn a great deal, they also need the money they make from racing.

4	

Gee Armitage, one of the relatively few women jockeys, is one who had a very serious fall some time ago and spent months in considerable pain.

5	

In spite of all her suffering, she was absolutely determined to return to the sport which she loved, although her friends and family wished that she would simply give it up.

6	

A As their passion for riding is so great, they do not worry greatly about how much money they make from the sport.

B "Jockeys are paid for every time they ride," said a race course doctor. "If I tell an injured jockey that he cannot ride in the following race, he loses money."

C Flat races take place in the summer months and are generally run over shorter distances than jump races. The emphasis is totally on speed.

D Although many people go to race meetings to bet money on which horses will win, others go to see the horses or simply because they enjoy the lively and exciting atmosphere.

E Even though jockeys are well aware of the dangers involved, they are usually keen to return to racing as soon as possible, even when their injuries have been very painful and serious.

F Gee says: "Racing is something you just can't give up. For a lot of us there are many more bad days than good days, but the good days are so good that they make up for the rest."

G In spite of this, the most famous horse race in Britain is a jump race called the Grand National. This takes place at Aintree in Liverpool every spring and attracts people from all over the world.

H She had been riding in a race at Huntingdon and her horse had been jumping perfectly but then fell badly at the next-to-last fence. Gee managed to get up and walk to the ambulance but was taken straight to hospital where she stayed for the next month.

Answers and notes on page 75.

LOOKING AT PART 4

In this part of the test you have a number of short questions followed by a number of short passages. Usually the passages will be separate articles on the same subject (e.g. advertisements for different cars, articles on the same story from different newspapers). Occasionally the passages may be different parts of one long passage. You have to find in which passage the answer to each question can be found.

ANSWERING THE QUESTIONS

Every question has a number and every passage has a letter. If, for example, you thought that the answer to question 33 was in passage D, you would mark letter D next to 33 on your answer sheet.

There will usually be between 13 and 15 questions and there may be as many as 9 passages (A, B, C, D, E, F, G, H, I), although there will often be fewer than this. Some of the passages will contain the answer to more than one question, so some of the letters will be used more than once. For example, if you had chosen D as the correct answer to question 33, this does not mean that D cannot be used again.

Sometimes the answer to a question can be found in two or even, occasionally, three of the passages. It is easy to know when this is going to happen as there will be two (or three) numbers beside the question. When you have found the two passages which contain the correct answer, you must mark them on the answer sheet. Here is an example of how a question like this appears on the paper:

Which articles are about a robbery?	32		33	

If you thought that the correct answers were in passages C and F, these are the letters you would mark on your answer sheet. When this happens, the order in which you put the letters does not matter, so you could mark the answer either as 32C 33F or 32F 33C.

The first question (which has the figure 0 at the beginning) is always an example and the answer is given for you, so be careful not to put the answer for 0 as your first answer.

APPEARANCE OF THE QUESTIONS

The first words of the questions may be the same for all questions and so these words are printed at the top of the question paper and only the remaining words of the question are placed by the numbers. If you are not clear what this means, look at several of the Practice Exercises and Exam Exercises 1, 3 and 4 for this part of the paper.

MULTIPLE CHOICE QUESTIONS

Sometimes there will be one or two questions at the end of this section which have multiple choice answers based on the passages. These questions may be of the type '*Who would find these passages interesting*?' '*In what kind of magazine might you find these advertisements?*'. (There are, in fact, no questions of this type in this book.)

CHOOSING THE BEST ANSWER

When you are looking for the passage containing the answer to a question, you may find that several of the passages contain parts of the answer. You must choose the passage which answers the question most fully.

Let us imagine that you had several passages about cars which were for sale and that one of the questions was:

Which car would be most suitable for someone wanting a large car less than five years old?

Passage A might mention 'a car which is three years old', passage B might mention 'a large car which is four years old'. You would, of course, choose passage B because this answers the question more fully than A (the car is large and less than five years old); passage A answers only part of the question – the car is less than five years old but we do not know if it is large or not.

Just occasionally you may find a question which is not completely answered in any of the passages. When this happens, you must choose the answer which gives the largest number of details. If the question had been:

Which car would be most suitable for someone wanting a large, blue car less than five years old?

and none of the passages mentioned a blue car, then B would still be the passage you would choose.

DIFFERENCE FROM PART 1

In Part 1 and Part 4 of this paper you have a similar matching task to do – in Part 1 you have to find a title or a summary which is suitable for one of several passages, in Part 4 you have to find the answer to a question in one of several passages. However, there is an important difference between the two parts – in Part 1 you are looking for a general understanding of the passages, in Part 4 you are looking for certain pieces of information. Part 1 is therefore testing general understanding, Part 4 is testing more detailed understanding.

PRACTICE EXERCISES

PRACTICE EXERCISE 1

Below are details of five pictures. Which picture would be most suitable for a person

1 who likes being on the coast?
2 who is interested in architecture?
3 who likes action?
4 who enjoys being in the countryside?
5 who is interested in clothes?

A a picture of a battle taking place
B a picture of a fashion show in Paris
C a picture of a ship leaving harbour
D a picture of a stream coming down a hill
E a picture of an old city

Now check your answers on page 75.

PRACTICE EXERCISE 2

Below are details of train and air services between London and the imaginary city of Melton. Which would be the best service (*train* or *air*) for somebody

1 who will be working in Melton until 6.00 p.m. before returning to London?
2 who wants to be in Melton by 9.30 a.m.?
3 who cannot afford to spend too much money?
4 who wants to arrive in Melton during the afternoon?
5 who likes to spend as little time as possible travelling?

TRAIN		**AIR**	
Time for the journey:	4 hours	Time for the journey:	1 hour
Time of first arrival in Melton:	10.30 a.m.	Time of first arrival in Melton	8.30 a.m.
Number of services daily:	6 throughout the day	Number of services daily:	1 in morning 1 in evening
Cost of return ticket:	£45	Cost of return ticket:	£120
Last departure from Melton:	7.30 p.m.	Last departure from Melton:	6.00 p.m.

Now check your answers on page 75.

PRACTICE EXERCISE 3

Below are two articles about the same road accident. Which article

1 tells us which hospital the accident victims were taken to?
2 tells us the jobs of the two people involved in the accident?
3 tells us most clearly where the accident happened?
4 tells us something of what happened when the victims were taken to hospital?
5 gives some information as to why the accident happened?

Article A: Two local residents were injured in a crash in front of Melton Town Hall shortly after 10.00 p.m. last night. The motorcyclist, Peter Johnson, a postman, skidded and hit the side of a car being driven by Louise Mason. The emergency services were soon on the scene and both were taken to hospital, where they were treated for shock. It is expected that both will be discharged later today.

Article B: An accident involving a motor cycle and a car happened in Melton last night. The road was very wet following heavy rain and the motor cycle skidded and hit the side of the car. The driver of the car, Louise Mason, a secretary from Melton, and the motor cyclist, Peter Johnson, a postman also from Melton, were both taken to Meadow Hill Hospital, where they were kept in overnight. It is not thought that either of them is seriously injured.

Now check your answers on page 75.

PRACTICE EXERCISE 4

Below are two newspaper articles about a new youth centre. Which article

1 gives some idea as to how soon the centre will be open?
2 gives the best idea of what will be available at the centre?
3 gives most information about opening times?
4 gives some suggestion as to why this centre is needed?
5 mentions an upper age limit?

Article A: A new youth centre is planned for Melton. The centre aims to cater for young people between the ages of 16 and 21. Initially the centre will be open only on Tuesdays, Thursdays, Fridays and Saturdays from 7.00 p.m., but if it proves to be successful, it is hoped to open the centre every night of the week. Young people wishing to become members will pay a small annual fee and will then be able to use all the facilities available. Activities will include discos, indoor games, speakers, excursions, etc.. The centre will have a bar serving soft drinks and snacks.

Article B: Plans for a new youth centre in Melton have been welcomed by local young people who have always complained that there is nothing for them in the town. The centre, which is due to open within the next two months, will provide a variety of activities from 7.00 p.m. on four nights every week. The centre will be open to all young people over 16 years of age on payment of an annual fee of £5.

Now check your answers on page 76.

PRACTICE EXERCISE 5

Below are brief details of three plays being shown on television. Which play would be most interesting for someone who

1 likes plays that have a happy ending?
2 likes plays that have a historical theme?
3 likes fast-moving plays?
4 likes romantic plays?
5 likes plays that are funny?

Talents: This play is set in the early years of the nineteenth century. It is based on the true story of the relationship between a teacher at one of the great English public schools and an exceptionally gifted pupil.

Patience: This is a modern-day love story in which a young couple from two different cultures meet by chance in a doctor's waiting room. It is a moving story, which traces the difficulties the couple have to overcome, but in the end all is well.

Arrest: This is a highly amusing detective story. There is plenty of action in the play as the police are constantly rushing in to arrest and then release one person after another. The ending of the play comes as a complete surprise.

Now check your answers on page 76.

PRACTICE EXERCISE 6

Below are details of three different eating places. Which of these eating places

1 is open for lunch?
2 sometimes provides music?
3 will serve you a drink without a meal?
4 says more about its setting than its food?
5 has fish as a speciality?

Beltons: Beltons is a beautiful restaurant serving food of the highest quality. We feel that a restaurant should provide not only excellent food but also an atmosphere of unhurried luxury. Take your time looking through the menu and enjoying the view of the nearby hills from our lounge windows, and then settle comfortably in our elegant dining room for a wonderful meal. Open every evening apart from Sundays.

Crawfords: Crawfords is renowned for its seafood, all of which is caught locally. We believe that all our dishes are of the highest quality but we are particularly proud of our chef's specialities based on sole and salmon. We are open every evening apart from Monday and have a live band playing for dancing on Friday and Saturday evenings.

Dooleys: Dooleys Café-Bar is situated in the centre of town and is the perfect place to call in if you feel like a light meal or just a drink. We serve a wide variety of soups, pancakes, sandwiches and cakes as well as the full range of alcoholic and soft drinks. We open every day at 11.00 a.m. and continue serving until 11.00 p.m..

Now check your answers on page 76.

PRACTICE EXERCISE 7

Below are details of three magazines. Which would be the most suitable magazine for someone

1 who is interested in finance?
2 who wants to read reports on cricket matches?
3 who is interested in what is happening in other countries?
4 who wants to be amused?
5 who is interested in the lives of famous people?

Weekly Review: Find out what has been happening to people in the public eye. You are sure to find this a fascinating magazine full of stories and photographs of stars from the worlds of television, films, sport and even politics! Every week we have interviews with at least two people about whom we are sure you will want to know more.

Weekly Post: A magazine which all the family can enjoy. Half the magazine is devoted to detailed coverage of all the major sports. The other half is full of cartoons and stories from all over Britain which are bound to make anybody laugh. Forget about all the problems in the world for a while and enjoy yourself with *Weekly Post.*

This Week: The magazine covers stories both at home and abroad. The main focus of the magazine is on politics and economics, although it also contains a page devoted to the Arts. Every week we have a detailed review of movements on the stock markets of the world and include up-to-the-minute advice on the latest investment schemes.

Now check your answers on page 76.

PRACTICE EXERCISE 8

Below are three articles about a new school science block. Which article tells us

1 why the science block has been named after Thomas Stanley?
2 something about how the school has coped since the fire?
3 most about the science block itself?
4 something of what Professor Walton had to say?
5 something about the attitude of the teachers?

Article A: The Thomas Stanley Science Centre at Melton School was officially opened yesterday by Sarah Walton, formerly a pupil at the school and now Professor of Theoretical Physics at an American university. The block consists of twelve laboratories for teaching Physics, Chemistry, Biology and Geology. The staff at the school are looking forward to working in an up-to-date centre after a difficult three years since fire destroyed several of the science laboratories in the school.

Article B: The new science block at Melton School was opened yesterday by Professor Sarah Walton, a former pupil of the school. The block will be known as the Thomas Stanley Science Centre in recognition of all the hard work put in by Mr Stanley, a former mayor of the town, in raising money for the building and equipping of the block. The school has been without full science facilities since a fire destroyed part of the buildings over three years ago.

Article C: Professor Sarah Walton yesterday opened the new science block at Melton school. Professor Walton, a former pupil at the school, spoke of the need for young people to leave school with a knowledge of science. The block consists of twelve laboratories and replaces the old laboratories which were destroyed in a fire some three years ago. Since the fire, many science lessons have had to take place either in ordinary classrooms or in the laboratories of the nearby Hill View School.

Now check your answers on page 76.

PRACTICE EXERCISE 9

Below are details of some young people who are looking for pen friends. Who would be the most suitable pen friend for a 14-year-old

1 girl who likes animals and is good at French at school?
2 boy who likes travelling and outdoor activities?
3 girl who likes going out and wants a boy for a pen friend?
4 boy who is keen on science at school and enjoys being in the countryside?
5 girl who loves children and enjoys shopping?

Peter: My name is Peter and I am a 14-year-old boy. I live in Leeds, which, as you probably know, is one of the largest cities in England. I am not really all that keen on school although I enjoy being with my friends there. It's good living in a big city like Leeds because there are lots of things to do. I often go out in the evenings and I really like going to the cinema or a disco when I've got enough money.

Sally: I am a 14-year-old girl and live just outside Bristol. I know the city quite well and I often go there to the cinema or to the shops. I am the oldest child in the family and have four little brothers and sisters. The two boys are 8 and 5 and the two girls are 10 and 3. They can be annoying sometimes but really we are all great friends. We have also got a dog and a cat.

Tim: I am a boy and am 14 years of age. I am the only child in the family. I quite like school, especially Physics and Chemistry. I enjoy travelling abroad even though I am no good at languages. I have been camping in France three times and I often go walking in the hills with my friends at weekends.

Jane: I am a girl and I had my fourteenth birthday last month. I live on a farm with my parents and my brother, who is four years older than me – we do not get on very well together. I have a dog who is great fun and I often go for long walks with him. I really enjoy school and my favourite subject is French.

Now check your answers on page 76.

PRACTICE EXERCISE 10

Below is some information for passengers arriving with British Airways at four airports in the United Kingdom.

1 Which airport is farthest from the city centre?
2 Which airport promises that it will not take long to get through the terminal?
3 Which airport has more than one terminal?
4 At which airport are there different levels for passengers arriving from abroad and those arriving from the UK?
5 Which airport provides a service which you do not have to pay for?

Manchester: Manchester is about 10 miles from the city centre. On arrival, passengers should report to the Connections Desk. Those connecting to British Airways international flights will then depart from Terminal 1 International. For those with connections to flights within the UK, the departure will be from Terminal 1 Domestic. Passengers connecting to other flights departing from Terminal 2 can take the free bus service which operates between the two terminals.

Birmingham: Birmingham Airport is about 8 miles from the city centre. All British Airways flights operate from Eurohub, a purpose-designed hub which ensures a quick and smooth journey through the terminal for all passengers. The modern design of Eurohub provides a pleasant, spacious environment offering high quality, efficient service.

Glasgow: Glasgow Airport is 8 miles from Glasgow city centre. Passengers on internal flights arrive at first floor level of the terminal. International passengers arrive at ground level. Passengers transferring to other flights should check with British Airways staff at the ground-floor ticket desk.

Edinburgh: Edinburgh Airport is 11 miles from Edinburgh city centre. The airport has a one-level arrivals area . Passengers should check on arrival with British Airways staff for connecting flights.

Now check your answers on page 76.

DOING THE EXAM

1 Read through the questions quickly to give you an idea of what you will be looking for.

2 Now read through the various passages quickly so that you have an idea of what the passages contain.

3 As you are reading through the passages, you may think you have already found the answers to some of the questions. However, do *not* begin to mark any of the answers on your answer sheet yet. You may *think* an answer is in one of the first passages but may then find a better and fuller answer in a later passage.

4 Read the example (question 0) and the passage from which it comes and try to understand why this is the correct answer.

5 Then read the first question and look through the passages until you find the one which contains the answer to the question. You may already have some idea of which passage to look at from your quick reading of the passages.

6 If you are unable to decide on an answer to the first question, do not spend too long reading through the passages but move on to the next question. (If you feel fairly certain that the answer is in two or three of the passages but you cannot decide which one, write down the letters for these passages on your question paper so that you know where to look when you return to this question later. However, do *not* write these letters on your answer sheet.)

7 Go through each question in the same way as you did with number 1. As you work through the test, you will probably begin to find it easier to find the answer because you are getting to know the passages better as you keep reading them.

8 When you have answered all the questions, go back to those which you have missed and try again to find the right answers.

Remember

- *Never* mark more than one letter for each number. (When there are two passages containing a correct answer to a question, the question will have two different numbers. When this happens, it does not matter in what order you put the numbers.)
- Some of the passages will be chosen more than once as they will contain the answer to more than one question.
- Do not choose a passage simply because it contains an unusual word which appears in the paragraph. This may be the right answer but it may also be wrong. Read the whole of the question and the whole of the passage.
- If you miss out an answer, make sure that when you put in the next answer, you put it by the correct number (that is to say that if, for example, you missed out answer 24, do not put answer 25 at the side of number 24).
- If you change your mind about an answer, remember to rub out the answer you had already indicated.
- Always mark one of the letters on the answer sheet even if, after thinking about the item, you are simply guessing the answer. There is always a chance that you may be right.

EXAM EXERCISES

EXAM EXERCISE 1

You are going to read some information about some properties which are for sale.
For questions **1-13**, choose from the properties (**A-I**). Some of the properties may be chosen more than once. When more than one answer is required, these may be given in any order. There is an example at the beginning (**0**).
For questions **14** and **15**, choose the answer (**A**, **B**, **C** or **D**) which you think is correct.

Which property or properties would you recommend for:

a single woman who travels a great deal in England and abroad ?	**0**	E
a young couple who have two dogs and are not very well off?	**1**	
a couple with a teenage son who are keen on improving old houses?	**2**	
a student without much money who often goes home to his parents?	**3**	
a well-off family with a grown up son and daughter living at home?	**4**	
two recently qualified nurses without a car?	**5**	
a couple with two children aged 7 and 9 who like to live in the city?	**6**	
a retired couple wanting an unhurried and peaceful life?	**7**	
a rich widow who enjoys city life and likes to have friends to stay?	**8**	
an unmarried airline pilot?	**9**	
a wealthy family who often entertain foreign guests on business?	**10**	
a quiet couple who work from home and enjoy long country walks ?	**11**	
people who like gardening but do not want to live in the countryside?	**12** / **13**	

14 Why would property E be *unsuitable* for who someone who finds it difficult to walk up stairs?
- **A** There is no lift.
- **B** The flat is on two floors.
- **C** The building is too high.
- **D** The kitchen is on the first floor.

15 Why is property F being offered at a reasonable price?
- **A** It needs some work doing on it.
- **B** It has recently been repaired.
- **C** The structure is not safe.
- **D** It does not sound secure.

Property A
An attractive semi-detached house built in 1990 consisting of dining room, lounge, kitchen, three bedrooms, bathroom. Large garden at rear of house and garage to the side. Situated in a quiet street in the centre of the city, the house is close to all the local shops and primary schools.

Property B
A magnificent detached house 12 kilometres from the city centre, less than 2 kilometres from the motorway and only 8 kilometres from the airport. The house consists of dining room, lounge, fitted kitchen, four bedrooms (two with their own bathrooms), one 'general' bathroom and a conservatory. Gardens to front and rear. Garage space for three cars. The property is surrounded by beautiful countryside with panoramic views of the nearby hills.

Property C
Small one-bedroom flat available above a clothes shop, consisting of one bedroom, kitchen and dining area, shared bathroom. The flat, which has gas central heating, is situated opposite the railway station and is convenient for all the facilities of the city.

Property D
A 2-bedroom house built in 1985 about 6 kilometres from the city centre. Dining area, kitchen, 2 bedrooms and bathroom. Garden at rear of house. Park and fields just a few minutes' walk from the house.

Property E
A luxury flat in a new development situated in a busy suburb of the city. The city centre, the airport and the motorway are all less than 15 minutes' drive away. The flat is on two levels on the ground floor and the first floor, and consists of dining area, kitchen, 1 bedroom and bathroom. Communal lawn with garage at the rear of the flat. Lovely views of the countryside from the front windows.

Property F
A 3-bedroom house built in 1952 about 8 kilometres from the city centre. The house is structurally sound but is being offered at a very reasonable price as it is in need of some internal modernising. The house consists of a dining room, lounge, kitchen, 3 bedrooms, bathroom. There is a garage at the side of the house and a small lawn to the rear. The local shops and schools are all within a 10-minute walk from the house.

Property G
A third-floor flat above an office block in the heart of the city. Dining area, kitchen, two bedrooms, bathroom. Access to the flat by private staircase. All the advantages of the city are close at hand. The flat faces the main bus station, making it easy to get to all parts of the city.

Property H
Delightful country cottage with fine views of hills and a nearby lake. Situated in the centre of a quiet village of about 600 people. The cottage consists of a large reception room, kitchen, 2 bedrooms, bathroom. There is a small garden at the front of the house and parking space at the side for one car. The cottage is close to the village shop and pub. A regular bus service operates between the village and the centre of the city, which is about 35 kilometres away.

Property I
A luxury flat on the third floor of a newly developed block in the city centre. The flat consists of a hall, lounge, dining room, fitted kitchen and two bedrooms, each with their own bathroom. Close to all the main facilities (shops, railway station, cinemas, theatres, art galleries, etc.) with magnificent views over the city. Gas central heating and lift.

Answers and notes on page 77.

EXAM EXERCISE 2

You are going to read some information about different jobs.
For questions **1-15**, choose from the jobs (**A-H**). Some of the jobs may be chosen more than once. When more than one answer is required, these may be given in any order. There is an example at the beginning (**0**).

Which job requires wide travel in the United Kingdom?	**0**	D		
Which job requires employees to call at customers' homes or firms?	**1**			
Which job lasts for only a few months?	**2**			
For which job is payment based on the age of the employee?	**3**			
For which job is it essential to know a foreign language?	**4**			
Which job would suit someone who likes to work alone?	**5**			
In which job will the successful applicant have to deal with the post?	**6**			
Which job would suit a person who likes being with old people?	**7**			
Which job requires the employee to work afternoons and evenings?	**8**			
Which job has a two-year training scheme?	**9**			
Which jobs state that the appearance of the employee is important?	**10**		**11**	
For which jobs is it essential for the candidate to be able to drive?	**12**		**13**	
Which jobs will require the person appointed to work abroad?	**14**		**15**	

Job A

Bettabuys supermarkets are looking for recruits for their management trainee scheme.

Candidates should have a recognised qualification in a relevant subject (e.g. management, economics, business studies). Experience in the retail trade is not essential as full training will be provided by the company.

Successful candidates will spend two years in a number of our branches learning all aspects of supermarket work. After this period of training, appointment as a deputy manager can be expected with promotion to manager when available.

Attractive salary during training with 4 weeks' holiday a year plus statutory holidays.

Job B

Wanderlust Holidays are looking for representatives to work in various European countries from mid-July until the end of October.

Representatives are responsible for ensuring the smooth running of our overseas holidays, for selling excursions and for dealing with complaints. Candidates should be lively and cheerful individuals who get on well with others. A knowledge of Spanish or Greek would be useful but is not essential.

Basic salary plus commission on excursions sold.

Job C

Oak Lodge provides care for elderly people in their own homes. We are seeking care staff to work either mornings or evenings. Experience is not essential as training is provided. A caring attitude and a sense of humour are far more important than paper qualifications.

Car and phone essential.

Payment by the hour to be discussed at interview.

Job D

PTI Medical Supplies are looking for representatives to work in all parts of the country. Representatives should have qualifications in the biological or medical fields and will need to have good communication skills. A current driving licence is essential.

Our representatives travel to different parts of the country to give demonstrations of our equipment to individual doctors and to medical and nursing staff at hospitals.

Highly attractive salary and car provided.

Job E

The *Wallgate Insurance Company* has a vacancy for a trainee insurance clerk.

Full training will be given, but applicants must have a good standard of education, be smart in appearance and be confident in dealing with members of the public face to face or over the telephone.

Salary dependent upon age and experience.

Job F

National Credit Bank is looking for recruits to its training scheme in its international branch.

The training scheme lasts for three years, during which all aspects of modern banking will be covered. In the first year training will take place at a local branch in Britain and at our staff college. For the following two years training will take place in a variety of different countries. At the end of the training, successful candidates can expect rapid promotion.

Applicants must have a knowledge of at least one foreign language and a qualification at degree level in a subject relevant to banking.

Job G

A vacancy has arisen for a receptionist at the show rooms of *Melton Cars.*

The successful applicant will be required to work from 2.00 p.m. to 8.00 p.m., Tuesdays to Saturdays.

This is a position which involves a great deal of telephone and face-to-face contact. The ideal candidate will be extremely smart, articulate, reliable and have a very pleasant personality. Duties will be quite varied, including dealing with incoming and outgoing mail. Typing skills would be a definite advantage.

In return we offer an attractive salary, excellent working conditions and the opportunity to develop with a major public company.

Job H

Hot Line Delivery gives you the possibility of working on a self-employed, part-time basis with one of the country's most successful parcel delivery services.

You will work on your own within a small geographical area, delivering and collecting parcels by car or van from customers' homes for around 15 to 20 hours per week, including some evenings as necessary.

If you are over 21, have your own transport and telephone, along with a polite manner to allow us to continue our reputation for professional quality customer service, phone us today.

Answers and notes on page 77.

EXAM EXERCISE 3

You are going to read some information about places where people can spend holidays. For questions **1-13**, choose from the holidays (**A-H**). Some of the holidays may be chosen more than once. When more than one answer is required, these may be given in any order. There is an example at the beginning (**0**).
For questions **14** and **15**, choose the answer (**A**, **B**, **C** or **D**) which you think is correct.

Which holiday would you recommend for:

two couples who enjoy country walks and touring in their cars?	**0**	C		
a young couple who want a break but who have very little money?	**1**			
a couple with two children aged 4 and 7?	**2**			
a single man with plenty of money who enjoys going to plays?	**3**			
two couples who want a reasonably cheap holiday by the seaside?	**4**			
a strong independent-minded girl who enjoys hard walking?	**5**			
a man without much money who gets bored on normal holidays?	**6**			
4 men who want to go fishing and not be tied down by meal times?	**7**			
a couple who like comfortable surroundings and enjoy dancing?	**8**			
a couple who like organised activities, preferably in the countryside?	**9**			
a rich widow wanting top class meals and accommodation?	**10**		**11**	
a well-off 30-year-old man who wants plenty to do on holiday?	**12**		**13**	

14 How many of these holidays offer accommodation at the seaside?
A 2 **B** 3 **C** 4 **D** 6

15 What do holidays C and H have in common?
A On both holidays various activities are organised.
B Both are near to a lot of villages.
C The bedrooms in both places are for two people.
D Both places are surrounded by hills.

Holiday A
Butlers Holiday Camp is designed for fun-loving young people. The camp is on the south coast and enjoys an enviable climate. Even if it does rain, there's no need to worry as there is plenty going on. Throughout the day you can swim in the pool, join in the organised games or take an excursion. In the evening there is always a mass of things to do – discos, talent contests, karaoke, etc. There is no age limit for this holiday but it is most likely to appeal to people aged between 20 and 35. Price per person per week for full board and entertainment programme £290.

Holiday B
Seaview Guest House is just a five-minute walk from the beach. There are five large family bedrooms and two bathrooms on each of the two floors. We give a warm welcome to everyone, but particularly enjoy having families with young children. Unfortunately, we cannot accept pets. Our terms include breakfast and a three-course evening meal. Price £95 per adult per week. Children under 16 £60. Children under 5 £20.

Holiday C
Swallow Cottage provides a self-catering holiday, perfect for anyone wanting to get away from it all and have a peaceful break in the heart of the English countryside. The cottage is in a valley surrounded by gentle hills. The area is perfect for anyone who wants to do a little gentle walking or to go fishing in the nearby river. For those who prefer to stay in their cars, there are many possibilities for delightful journeys around the country lanes and surrounding villages. The cottage consists of a dining area, kitchen, two bedrooms, bathroom. Rental £350 per week.

Holiday D
For the dedicated walker, Rangers Mountain Lodge offers the perfect holiday. Situated 1,000 metres above sea-level, the lodge offers wonderful views over the mountains with unsurpassed possibilities for hiking and rock climbing. The lodge is not luxurious but it offers clean and comfortable accommodation, plentiful meals and, most important of all, bracing mountain air. Price £20 per night (breakfast included).

Holiday E
Sheldon House is a hotel which caters for people who expect quality and are not prepared to put up with second best. The hotel dominates the town and guests can enjoy marvellous views out to sea from our sun lounge. The hotel has a fitness centre and both outdoor and indoor swimming pools for the exclusive use of residents. We provide a full English breakfast and a magnificent five-course evening meal with wine included. Every evening after dinner there is dancing to our resident three-piece band. Gentlemen are requested to wear ties in the dining room. Costs for accommodation, breakfast and evening meal from £95 per person daily.

Holiday F
Why not earn some money and have a holiday surrounded by beautiful countryside at the same time? Maybury farm camp offers you the possibility to do just that. During your time with us you will be accommodated in chalets for two people. Breakfast, a picnic lunch and a hearty evening meal are included. The bar is open every evening and we often have dancing to tapes. On five days of every week you will be taken to local farms for fruit picking. It is impossible to say how much you will earn but most campers more than cover the cost of the holiday. Price £80 per week.

Holiday G
Sanders is a four-star hotel in the centre of Melton, a city only 30 kilometres from the coast. The hotel prides itself on the excellence of its accommodation and food. All bedrooms have bath, toilet, television, hair dryer and tea-making facilities. Dining in our beautiful restaurant is an experience in itself but if sometimes you do not feel like coming down to the restaurant, meals can be served in your room at any time of day or night. You will find all the advantages of being in a large city so close at hand – theatres, art galleries, shops and the magnificent Cathedral are all just a few minutes' walk away from the hotel. Price per night including breakfast and evening dinner £120 per person.

Holiday H
The Walton Club welcomes people who want an active holiday in the countryside. Situated in the midst of rolling hills 20 kilometres from the city of Melton, the club welcomes anyone from the age of 21. Every day we organise a wide variety of activities including golf, hang gliding, horse riding, canoeing, dancing, walking. Accommodation is in twin-bedded rooms, all with shower and w.c.. Cost £320 per week covering accommodation and full board (activities extra).

Answers and notes on page 78.

EXAM EXERCISE 4

You are going to read some information about several films.

For questions **1-15**, choose from the films (**A-H**). Some of the films may be chosen more than once. When more than one answer is required, these may be given in any order. There is an example at the beginning (**0**).

Which film or films:

is about a person who moves to another part of the country for work?	**0**	C		
concerns people for whom work is the only thing that matters?	**1**			
has all the action taking place in a period of less than 24 hours?	**2**			
has people bringing different values to another community?	**3**			
is successful largely because of a young actress?	**4**			
has a young woman mixing with women much older than herself?	**5**			
began life as a play in the theatre?	**6**			
shows how a new situation can change a person's character?	**7**			
has people speaking of things they would normally not speak about?	**8**			
might be rather dull if it were not for the scenery in it?	**9**			
is about two men in love with another man's wife?	**10**			
was made over 40 years ago?	**11**			
from what we read, does not contain a romantic or love theme?	**12**		**13**	
involves a person going abroad after a death?	**14**		**15**	

Film A

Stealing Beauty is a moving and often very amusing film, which owes its charm to an intelligent script and a magnificent performance by Liv Tyler. In the film 19-year-old Lucy, played by Tyler, moves from the USA, following the death of her mother, to stay with family friends in a farmhouse in Italy. The house is owned by Ian Grayson, an artist, who is to paint her portrait. Lucy, however, has a hidden agenda; she wants to see the boy she fell in love with four years earlier and to learn the identity of her real father, clues to which lie in one of the poems written by her mother.

Film B

August is set in a country house in North Wales during the late 19th century when a group of people gather at the home of the Davis family. The visitors are the tyrannical Professor Alexander Blathwaite, the absentee owner of the estate, and his second wife, the much younger American, Helen. They waste little time in imposing their London ways on the rural inhabitants, including Ieuan, brother of Blathwaite's first wife, and the professor's plain daughter, Sian. Ieuan falls passionately in love with Helen although she shows no interest in him. Sian conceals a secret love for the local doctor, Michael Lloyd, who is also in love with Helen. Ieuan tries to find comfort in drink and, in a series of tragi-comic episodes, the ordered calm of the household begins to disintegrate.

Film C
Dead Man is a cowboy film with a difference, breathtakingly shot in black and white. In the film William Blake, an honourable accountant, has come to the west to take up a job which fails to materialise. A stranger in town, he finds himself alone and without money, and so begins a chain of encounters which lead this law-abiding citizen into crime. The central theme of the film is that life is unpredictable and that unexpected circumstances can completely change the course of a person's life.

Film D
Denise Calls Up is a funny and thoroughly modern story about a group of young Americans whose lives are based totally on work. Their days consist of talking on mobile phones, answering faxes and watching computer screens. Lunch dates are made and missed, parties are organised but never attended, and the friends even fail to turn up at the funeral of one of their pals (killed in a car accident while talking on her car phone). Then along comes Denise, an outsider to the group. She has an urgent personal problem, but will she be able to find enough time in her busy schedule to deal with it?

Film E
A Month by the Lake is based loosely on a romantic story by H.E.Bates. In the film Vanessa Redgrave plays Miss Bentley, an independent and impetuous middle-aged woman, who travels to a resort by Lake Como in Italy following the death of her father in 1935. There she meets and falls in love with fellow holidaymaker Major Wilshore, an eccentric but likeable man. After various unsuccessful dates, it seems unlikely that the romance will ever really get going until a couple of other people begin to show more than a passing interest in the pair. If the film is unremarkable in its content, it makes good use of its beautiful Italian locations.

Film F
The oddly named *How to make an American Quilt* tells the story of Finn, an American graduate student, who heads off to spend her summer vacation with her grandmother and great grandmother. Soon she is introduced to a group of elderly ladies who spend much of their time together sewing. The work they are producing is useful for her studies on women's handicrafts but the stories Finn is told about their youth, family histories, loves and marriages soon prove far more interesting than their sewing skills. Meanwhile her own love life is in difficulty as she cannot choose between her good, reliable boyfriend and an incredibly attractive newcomer.

Film G
Two Deaths is a film in which all the action takes place within a single eventful night. In Bucharest in 1989 a collection of guests gather at the home of the wealthy, mysterious Dr Pavenic. When they are settled over a lavish dinner, the doctor reveals that he is madly in love with his housekeeper and tells his guests of the lengths he has gone to in order to make her return his attention. Encouraged by this revelation, the guests also begin to reveal their own secrets and desires. As the dinner party continues, civil war breaks out in the city and soldiers from the opposing sides enter the house.

Film H
The film of *The Philadelphia Story* was based on a stage play which had been written especially for the actress Katharine Hepburn. The story begins shortly before a high society wedding between the lively Tracy Lord and her dull fiancé, George. Invitations have been sent out, gifts received, the reception organised and the family assembled. Indeed, everything seems perfect until Tracy's ex-husband and a reporter and photographer from a magazine turn up. The film was one of the best loved and most charming comedies of the 1940s and was later turned into the still more successful musical *High Society*.

Answers and notes on page 78.

Trial Paper A

You have 1 hour and 15 minutes in which to complete this test.

PART 1

You are going to read an article about problems that some students have. Choose the most suitable heading from the list **A-H** for each part (**1-6**) of the article. There is one extra heading which you do not need to use. There is an example at the beginning (**0**).
Mark your answers **on the separate answer sheet.**

A University's lack of concern

B Reaction of students

C What use are the extra facilities?

D Problems exaggerated

E Impossible to keep clean

F Lack of accommodation

G Water to be restored soon

H Week with no hot water

Answers and notes for Trial Paper A are on page 79.

PROBLEM FOR STUDENTS

0	H

Students paying more than £700 a term for better quality accommodation in a university hall of residence have been left without hot water for a week. More than sixty students at Lonsdale University's Miller Park complex have been affected after water pipes burst.

1	

The students say that even though supplies were restored, many have been without water. Some students are missing lectures because they have gone back to stay with their parents until the problem is put right. Others are paying to use sports facilities just to use the showers.

2	

One student said: "Dishes are piling up in sinks, and we can't even have a wash. I work at night in a local pub and after spending hours in a smoky atmosphere, I have to go into lectures without being able to clean up.

3	

"We have made repeated complaints to the university but they don't appear interested. Somebody actually told us to stop making a fuss. Everybody else locally had water supplies back on by Friday last week after the burst, but it was really late on Sunday before we even had cold water running.

4	

"We couldn't flush the toilets and people were having to buy bottled water just to make a cup of tea. We're paying extra for luxuries like showers in our rooms but we can't even use them.

5	

"Somebody has said if they can't sort out this problem, the university will have to find alternative accommodation, but how are they going to do that for 64 students at this stage of the term?"

6	

A university spokesman said: "Obviously we apologise to the students for the inconvenience but this was a major burst that affected households in the area as well as halls of residence and we reacted as swiftly as we could. Not all flats were without hot water in Miller Park and the situation in relation to those that were has now been dealt with."

PART 2

You are going to read an article about the Irish language. For questions **7-14**, choose the answer (**A**,**B**,**C** or **D**) which you think fits best according to the text.
Mark your answers **on the separate answer sheet**.

THE IRISH LANGUAGE TODAY

Until about the seventeenth century, Irish was the normal everyday language of Ireland. At that time, though, the English who had colonised the country began to impose their own language and the Irish people gradually accepted this, mostly for economic reasons. All official business was conducted in English and the British economy dominated the country. This practical motivation to use English grew even stronger when people began to leave Ireland in vast numbers in the nineteenth century. Families thought that it would be difficult to move to an English-speaking country such as America, Australia or England if they knew nothing but Irish.

Nowadays it is estimated that little more than one per cent of the population of the country use Irish as their daily first language. Even in the areas of the country which are supposed to be Irish-speaking, the use of the language is decreasing. These areas, known officially as the 'Gaeltacht', are mainly in the remote far west of the country and have a total population of 83,000, of whom nearly all can speak Irish, although only about 30,000 use it as their normal language of communication.

All children in Ireland have to learn Irish. Until 1973 pupils had to gain a pass in Irish if they were to be awarded their school leaving certificate. This rule was very unpopular and was dropped. Pupils still have to take Irish for these examinations but it no longer seems to matter very much if they fail.

Most children in primary schools seem to enjoy their Irish lessons but in secondary schools the situation is often different. As examination pressure mounts, pupils often find Irish to be boring and irrelevant, as compared with French or German, which can at least be useful for getting a job.

The most surprising development of recent years has been the rapid rise in the number of state schools in towns that do all their main teaching in Irish. This is not a scheme imposed by the state but one that has grown up in response to the demands of parents. Some parents send their children to these schools for patriotic reasons, believing them to be a defence against the country being swamped with American and English culture. Many other parents choose these schools simply because they see them as being better than the English-language schools. They tend to be newer and to have smaller classes and better motivated teachers. One criticism made of these schools is that they could be distracting pupils from learning 'more useful' modern languages. In fact, in modern languages, as in most subjects, these schools have results which are better than the national average.

Only time will tell whether the new rise in Irish in the towns will compensate for its decline in the Irish-speaking areas of the rural west.

7 What do we learn in this passage about Ireland at the beginning of the seventeenth century?
- **A** Many people left for America, Australia and England.
- **B** English had always been the language used in business.
- **C** The British began to invade the country.
- **D** People spoke Irish as their everyday language.

8 People who left Ireland thought
- **A** they needed nothing more than Irish.
- **B** they would find life easy in an English-speaking country.
- **C** they ought to know some English.
- **D** they should pretend not to be Irish.

9 In the 'Gaeltacht'
- **A** 83,000 people use Irish as their normal language of communication.
- **B** almost everybody uses Irish as their first language.
- **C** 30,000 people do not understand Irish.
- **D** there is a fall in the number of people using Irish as their first language.

10 Since 1973 pupils in Irish schools
- **A** have not needed to pass Irish in order to gain their school leaving certificate.
- **B** have had to drop Irish.
- **C** have needed to pass Irish in order to gain their school leaving certificate.
- **D** have not had to study Irish.

11 Why are French and German often more popular than Irish in secondary schools?
- **A** They ensure that pupils can find a job.
- **B** They are not boring.
- **C** They can help pupils find work.
- **D** They ease examination pressure.

12 The government introduced schools where teaching was done in Irish because
- **A** they have better results.
- **B** parents wanted them.
- **C** pupils in towns do not learn Irish.
- **D** the teachers are more committed

13 Some people have criticised these Irish language schools because
- **A** they prevent pupils from learning modern languages.
- **B** they have classes which are too small.
- **C** their results are only a little better than average.
- **D** they do not teach any useful subjects.

14 Which of the following would make a suitable title for this passage?
- **A** Irish – End in Sight.
- **B** Irish – Signs of Hope in the Towns.
- **C** Irish – A Dead Language.
- **D** Irish – Increasingly Important in the Villages.

PART 3

You are going to read a newspaper article about an English seaside resort. Seven sentences have been removed from the article. Choose from the sentences A-H the one which fits each gap (15-20). There is one extra paragraph which you do not need to use. There is an example at the beginning (0).
Mark your answers on the separate answer sheet.

BLACKPOOL

Many English people now go abroad for their holidays in search of better weather.
0 G By far the biggest of these resorts is Blackpool, which still welcomes some six million visitors every year.

At the beginning of the 19th century, Blackpool was a little-known fishing village on the north-west coast of England with a population of fewer than 500. **15** _____ This gave the inhabitants of these towns the chance to get away from their smoke-filled environment and seek fresh air on the coast.

The visitors soon began to demand organised entertainment and Blackpool was quick to oblige. **16** _____ The tower was built in imitation of the Eiffel Tower in Paris, even though it is hardly half the height of the French original. Nevertheless, for many years it was Britain's tallest structure. The Tower contained a highly decorated ballroom and the Tower Circus.

Along a large part of the seafront is the so-called *Golden Mile*, a lively area of hot-dog stands, amusement arcades and fortune tellers. At the southern end of the seafront stands the vast Pleasure Beach, full of exciting rides and more amusement arcades. The Pleasure Beach, which has more visitors every year than any other tourist attraction in Britain, has provided Blackpool with a second tower. **17** _____

One of the principal attractions of Blackpool to many people is the trams which run along the seafront. **18** _____ However, in recent years several cities have re-introduced trams on to their streets.

Blackpool has the longest holiday season of any seaside town in Britain. **19** _____ From early September until the end of October, crowds come in their thousands to see the *Illuminations,* when the seafront is transformed into a glittering display of coloured lights and scenes, with trams disguised as moon rockets and American showboats.

Blackpool is not to everyone's taste but it is a town with a basic honesty. **20** _____

A Theatres and dance halls were quickly provided for the holidaymakers, but the most striking building was Blackpool Tower, which was erected between 1891 and 1894.

B Whilst summer is, no doubt, the busiest time of year, conferences and exhibitions take place in spring and autumn.

C However, others continue to go to the traditional English seaside resorts.

D This was the first tower to be built in Blackpool and dates back to the time when the town was just a fishing village.

E It does not claim to be smart and sophisticated but simply a place where people can come and have fun.

F This is a 50-metre-high column called the *Space Tower,* which an observation car ascends to give a panoramic view of the coastline.

G For many years these were the only commercial trams still operating in Britain.

H The arrival of the railways in 1846 linked Blackpool with the industrial towns in the counties of Lancashire and Yorkshire.

PART 4

You are going to read some information about some schools.
For questions **21-33**, choose from the schools (**A-G**). Some of the schools may be chosen more than once. When more than one answer is required, these may be given in any order. There is an example at the beginning (**0**).
For questions **34** and **35**, choose the answer (**A**, **B**, **C** or **D**) which you think is correct.
Mark your answers **on the separate answer sheet**.

Which school or schools would be most suitable for:

a girl who wants to do well in languages?	**0**	E		
a shy and quiet boy who enjoys painting?	**21**			
a girl who is not very clever but who wants to learn to play the flute?	**22**			
a boy who is keen on Chemistry and enjoys singing?	**23**			
a girl who likes sport and helping people?	**24**			
a boy who likes animals?	**25**			
a girl who wants to be an actress?	**26**			
a boy who is keen on sport and wants to go on to university?	**27**			
a girl who is keen to study Physics and Chemistry?	**28**		**29**	
a boy who enjoys music and travelling?	**30**		**31**	
a girl who prefers not to be near the centre of town?	**32**		**33**	

34 How many of the schools refer to rules about the clothes pupils should wear?
A 1 **B** 2 **C** 3 **D** 5

35 What do schools B and C have in common?
A Both are near the town centre.
B Both are about the same size.
C Both schools accept boys.
D Both are highly academic.

SCHOOL A

We are a mixed school in the centre of town and have just under 1,700 pupils aged from 11 to 18 on our rolls. The teaching staff numbers over a hundred. As a large school, we are able to provide pupils with a wide range of courses as well as a wealth of out-of-school activities.

We believe that teaching in all subjects is of a high standard but we are particularly proud of our examination results in science. Well equipped laboratories complement the good teaching and every year a large proportion of our sixth form pupils proceed to university to study science subjects.

The school also has a strong musical tradition. The choir and orchestra perform several concerts annually and last year the orchestra toured Germany, giving seven performances in four different towns.

SCHOOL B

We are a boys' school of 400 pupils from the age of 11 to 16. The school is situated on the outskirts of the town. We offer courses in all the usual school subjects but are particularly committed to Art.

Although we are, of course, concerned with the academic success of our pupils, our main aim is to be a caring community in which all boys, whether gifted or not, can feel secure. We do not claim to send vast numbers of our pupils to university but we do try to ensure that pupils leave the school as well-balanced young people ready to play a responsible part in society.

SCHOOL C

We are a medium sized boys' school of 750 pupils from the age of 11 to 16. The school, which is about five kilometres from the centre of town, stands in a beautiful situation surrounded on all sides by open countryside. We take advantage of our situation by having a farm unit where we have a number of hens, pigs and sheep.

Music is important in the life of the school, as are trips abroad: last year parties from the school visited France, Spain, Denmark and the USA.

SCHOOL D

We are a small girls' school situated in a quiet suburb about two kilometres from the town centre. There are about four hundred pupils in the school, with ages ranging from 11 to 16.

All the normal school subjects are offered and in addition all pupils are required to learn a musical instrument. Whilst we want our pupils to succeed academically, our main aim is to produce young women who are well-balanced and keen to play a part in the life of the community.

SCHOOL E

We are a medium sized girls' school in the centre of town, with 700 pupils on our rolls from the age of 11 to 18. The school has a reputation for high academic standards and the majority of our pupils proceed to university after finishing their school career.

Examination results in languages and the sciences are particularly impressive. All pupils are required to study two foreign languages up to GCSE level. Latin is an optional extra.

We expect parents to encourage their daughters to work hard and to adhere to the school's dress code.

SCHOOL F

We are an all boys' school taking pupils from the age of 11 to 18. Last year we had 682 pupils on our rolls. Sport plays an important part in the life of the school; for the last three years our rugby team has won the county championship trophy for schools.

Many of our pupils go on to university after school. We do not single out success in any particular subjects as being impressive, as we think our standards are impressive in all subjects.

SCHOOL G

We are a large school of 1,500 pupils, about 3 kilometres from the centre of town. Pupils join the school at the age of 11 and may remain with us until they are 18. We have a large sports field and have an enviable record of sporting successes. We do not make distinctions between the sexes in sport: girls may play football if they wish, boys may play netball.

The school has its own purpose-built theatre and we are proud of the standard of music and drama in the school. We produce a minimum of two plays and one musical every year. In addition, all pupils in the first three years have at least one hour of music and drama every week.

The school is aware of its responsibilities to the wider community and organises various activities for old people in the town. A major fund-raising event is also held annually, the proceeds of which go to a national charity chosen by the pupils.

Trial Paper B

You have 1 hour and 15 minutes in which to complete this test.

PART 1

You are going to read an article about a cookery course. Choose from the list **A-H** the sentence which best summarises each part (**1-6**) of the article. There is one extra sentence which you do not need to use. There is an example at the beginning (**0**)
Mark your answers **on the separate answer sheet**.

A The course shows you only the way dishes are prepared in this restaurant.

B We ate some of the food we had prepared.

C None of the people on the course was a professional cook.

D Restaurant work is hard and tiring for the kitchen staff.

E There was a different theme for each day.

F It was interesting to find out what the other people on the course were like.

G We all sat at the same table for huge evening meals accompanied by champagne.

H The course was not intended for people who were basically wanting a holiday.

Answers and notes for Trial Paper B are on page 81.

A COOKERY COURSE

0	H

I have never been a person who is at his best in the morning. I do not really begin to take much interest in the day until 11.00 a.m.. The cookery course I attended made no concessions to my wish for a late start. The schedule tended towards work camp rather than leisure break, with breakfast served at 8.00 and a punctual start at 8.30 every morning.

1	

Of the eight pupils around the breakfast table on the first morning, all, including me, were amateur cooks who had come to the course with the intention of extending their range of skills.

2	

We had all been introduced on the previous evening at a meeting with Clive, the head chef at the hotel where the course was taking place. Each day was designed to show us different methods and approaches for different parts of a meal. The first day would concentrate on hot and cold starters, the second on fish, the third on meat and the final day on desserts.

3	

One of the first lessons for a student with ambitions of opening a restaurant is to observe Clive and his team in action. Lessons take place right in the middle of their working kitchen. The hours are long, the work exhausting and the standards exceptionally high.

4	

Organised into pairs, we watched Clive's demonstrations and then tried to imitate what he had done. Occasionally one of the students would talk about the way they prepared a dish at home, or mention a method they had read or heard about somewhere. The response was always the same: "Our aim is to show you how we do it here".

5	

Exhausted at the end of the day, we had a couple of hours to rest before the evening meal. All the students sat around the same table, although it was possible to reserve a table for oneself if one wanted to, but part of the enjoyment of the course was in discovering the characters of one's fellow students.

6	

The final evening, after a champagne reception at which we were presented with our certificates for completing the course, we sat down to an eight-course meal. One element of this was the product of our own labours, a magnificent chocolate dessert. And, although I say it myself, mine was absolutely delicious.

PART 2

You are going to read an article about going to the library in the past. For questions **7-14**, choose the answer (**A**, **B**, **C** or **D**) which you think fits best according to the text.
Mark your answers **on the separate answer sheet**.

GOING TO THE LIBRARY IN THE PAST

When I go into our local library, I often watch children looking at the shelves filled with a variety of brightly coloured books. They pick a book, glance through a few of the pages and then almost immediately reject it before beginning to look at another book. I smile to myself for when I was a child in the 1910s, we were never allowed anywhere near the books. They were kept in some remote corner of the building to which only the librarian had access.

How, you may ask, did we manage to choose the book which we wanted to borrow? Well, immediately to the right of the entrance was a room which served two purposes: it was a reading room for the older members of the community and it contained catalogues in alphabetical order of the titles and authors of the books kept in the library. Using these, all one had to do was to write out a list of the books required. However, since most of us knew very few authors by name, and even fewer book titles, the whole process of borrowing a book was based upon guesses. There was no possibility of looking through the first few pages to help us form an opinion, no looking at illustrations to discover if a book might arouse our interest.

Even now I recall almost with pain some of the selections my friends and I made. We learned with dismay that titles often gave little guidance as to what the book was about. If we could have returned the book the next day, our irritation would have been considerably reduced, but this was not possible. The librarian did not allow us to bring back any book until we had kept it for at least a week.

Having written out your list, you presented it to the librarian. If you thought your troubles were finished, you were sadly mistaken. Your hands were inspected to make sure they were clean. More than once, one or other of us was sent out of the library and told to return when we had washed our hands.

Once the librarian was satisfied that we were clean enough, she would disappear into another room and return with the first book on our list which was available. When a book was returned, she would make a thorough inspection of the pages to make sure that it had not been damaged in any way. At least that way we never got blamed for something we had not done.

Although the librarian appeared very strict and frightening to a small boy, I owe her and the man who gave the library to the town an immense debt of gratitude. They led me into the land of story, romance and adventure, which in years to come brightened many a dull day.

7 According to the first paragraph, how is life different for children today from life for children in the 1910s?
- **A** They always get what they want.
- **B** They have a wider choice of books.
- **C** They are allowed to behave badly.
- **D** They spend more time reading books.

8 It was difficult for children to know which books to choose because
- **A** there was no list of authors.
- **B** the illustrations did not interest them.
- **C** there were only a few book titles.
- **D** they could not see the books in advance.

9 How did children find out which books were available in the library?
- **A** They had to write out a list.
- **B** They had to ask the librarian.
- **C** They had to look through the catalogues.
- **D** They had to order them.

10 What does the writer say about book titles?
- **A** Nobody knew any of them.
- **B** They told us what books were about.
- **C** There were not very many of them.
- **D** They were not very helpful.

11 What rule was there about returning a book to the library?
- **A** You had to keep it until the following day.
- **B** You had to return it within a week.
- **C** You had to keep it for a week or more.
- **D** You had to return it by the following day.

12 What did the librarian do as soon as she had received a child's list?
- **A** She looked at the children's hands.
- **B** She sent all the children away to wash their hands.
- **C** She washed the children's hands.
- **D** She asked the children if their hands were dirty.

13 Why does the author think that it was a good idea for the librarian to check the books carefully when they were returned?
- **A** She would be able to find out why you had damaged the book.
- **B** You would not be accused of damaging a book that was already damaged.
- **C** She would be able to find out if somebody else had damaged the book.
- **D** You would not be blamed if you had damaged a book.

14 Why is the writer grateful to the librarian?
- **A** She helped open up the world of literature to him.
- **B** She told him wonderful stories.
- **C** She helped to cheer him up when he was older.
- **D** She made him feel like an adult.

PART 3

You are going to read a newspaper article about a person who had to catch a plane. Seven paragraphs have been removed from the article. Choose from the paragraphs **A-H** the one which fits each gap (**15-20**). There is one extra paragraph which you do not need to use. There is an example at the beginning (**0**).
Mark your answers **on the separate answer sheet**.

A LUCKY PASSENGER

An airline pilot with a long piece of string opened the cockpit window on his plane to reunite a passenger with her lost spectacles, just a few moments before taking off from Heathrow Airport, London.

0	G

The passenger, Susan Schwartz, had left her glasses at terminal four of the airport after she landed on a flight from Philadelphia in the United States.

15	

Ms Schwartz informed a member of the British Airways staff, who contacted staff in the other terminal. A frantic search began for the glasses.

16	

As the Milan flight with its 250 passengers, including Ms Schwartz, drew away from its stand, all seemed lost.

17	

Nevertheless, the British Airways customer-service agent at Heathrow, Bob Hughes, contacted the flight by radio and rushed across the runway by car.

18	

A British Airways spokesman said: “Of course, the plane’s stairs had been removed. Captain Swift suddenly had an idea and managed to get hold of a long piece of string”.

19	

“He told the passengers what was happening and a lot of them watched out of the window as the glasses were attached to the string and pulled up,” said the British Airways spokesman.

20	

A A three-way conversation took place between Mr Hughes, traffic controllers and Captain Brian Swift on board the aircraft about how to get the glasses on board the plane.

B "One who did not watch was Ms Schwartz. We understand that she is rather short-sighted."

C She had had to go from terminal four to terminal one in order to catch her onward flight to Milan but, once there, she realised that she had left her glasses at the other terminal.

D Suddenly, the glasses were found, but by then the plane was over a kilometre away from the terminal and was fifth in line for take-off.

E A few moments after the plane had taken off, the glasses were pulled on to the plane by two passengers sitting near Ms Schwartz.

F Time was beginning to run out and Ms Schwartz, along with the other passengers, was taken by bus to the aircraft.

G Air traffic controllers kept an eye on what was happening on the runway as a car rushed past lines of planes waiting to take off.

H The glasses were pulled aboard from 5 metres below, just in time for Captain Swift to close the small side cockpit window and head for take-off without missing his place in the queue.

PART 4

You are going to read some information about various types of entertainment which were taking place in Britain one summer.
For questions **21-35**, choose from the different types of entertainment available (**A-I**). Some of the entertainments may be chosen more than once. When more than one answer is required, these may be given in any order. There is an example at the beginning (**0**).

Mark your answers **on the separate answer sheet**.

Which entertainment or entertainments:

requires cars to be banned from a street on one day?	**0**	G
would seem to be the most dangerous?	**21**	
involves a theatre that can be moved about?	**22**	
features a person who is annoyed for a time and then pleased?	**23**	
is about a person failing to find what he is looking for?	**24**	
is about a person in space?	**25**	
will contain songs which were recently recorded?	**26**	
contains a high-speed journey?	**27**	
is concerned with the effect of becoming suddenly rich?	**28**	
features large model animals?	**29**	
deals with the life of someone who lived over a hundred years ago?	**30**	
is concerned with a writer's memories of his past?	**31**	
is particularly suitable for children?	**32**	**33**
deals with the problem of feeling lonely?	**34**	**35**

ENTERTAINMENT A

Manchester's Royal Exchange Company will take its production of *Tess of the d'Urbervilles* on tour throughout the country. The play, based on the novel by Thomas Hardy, has Nelli Garnett in the title role.

The Royal Exchange mobile theatre, a replica of the ground floor level of the company's home theatre-in-the-round in Manchester, will be erected in sports and leisure centres around the country.

ENTERTAINMENT B

Jackson Browne, whose folk rock songs reflect his strong views on social and environmental issues, will be on tour in the UK this summer performing songs from his latest album *Looking East*. In addition to a solo career, Browne has worked with *The Eagles*, co-writing several of their early songs.

ENTERTAINMENT C

Reaching heights of over 10 metres above the audience's heads, and without safety nets, Momentary Fusion performs its blend of aerial acrobatics and physical theatre, described as 'anti-gravity dance', in a show called *Stung*. The show explores the themes of solitude and fear, with the three-strong company performing on swinging ropes.

ENTERTAINMENT D

This year's York Early Music Festival focuses on the last ten years of each century from the Middle Ages to the present day. Taking advantage of the wide variety of historic buildings around the city, the 10-day festival opens in York Minster with the world premiere of a children's opera.

ENTERTAINMENT E

Steve Steen is to go on tour with his one-man adaptation of Bill Bryson's book *The Lost Continent*. Steen plays Bryson returning to the land of his youth in search of the perfect American small town. The territory is known to him only from the films of his youth and childhood holidays spent travelling across the States, and he is bemused to find strip after strip of identical motels and hamburger outlets. Seeing the friendliness he remembers turned to hard sell and neon lights, Bryson is forced to admit that he has become a foreigner in his own country.

ENTERTAINMENT F

The third Barclays New Stages Festival takes place in Birmingham this year with a varied programme of new work. There is a selection of dance events including the Motionhouse Dance Company in collaboration with the Birmingham Contemporary Music Group in the show *Delicate*, which follows six characters in their efforts to find a cure for loneliness.

The acclaimed company *Candoco*, a group of able-bodied and disabled dancers, presents *A Flock Apart*. At Cannon Hill Park there will be a performance of *7/8 of a Second*, a combination of music, video, dance and fireworks, while *Stan's Café* will stage the first performance of its new play *Ocean of Storms*, in which an astronaut is trapped in orbit around the earth.

ENTERTAINMENT G

The focus of Islington's second festival is on Upper Street, which will be closed to traffic for the final day of the festival. Among the artists to be seen will be *Totem*, from Belgium, with giant wooden camels, while leading exponents of street performance, *The Natural Theatre Company* and *Desperate Men and Women*, are also due to appear. The *Grand Union Orchestra* will be playing on a huge stage outside the Town Hall, and the work of more than 40 artists will be featured in shop fronts on Upper Street.

ENTERTAINMENT H

The *Pop-up Touring Company* is taking its show *Iron Dreams* around Great Britain this summer, using its own blend of visual imagery, physical performance and music to tell the story of the 19th century engineer Isambard Kingdom Brunel through the eyes of a child. The show, suitable for anyone over six years of age, covers the launch of the ship *SS Great Britain*, the opening of the Thames tunnel and a break-neck steam train ride from London to Bristol.

ENTERTAINMENT I

In its 25th anniversary year, Hull Truck Theatre Company is to tour the first ever stage play about the National Lottery. This is a satirical comedy about the effects on a family of becoming overnight millionaires.

In the play, Morris, a security guard, carefully chooses the lottery numbers each week, and his wife buys the tickets. His anger when she picks her own combination of numbers one week soon subsides upon finding that they have won

Answers and Notes

2 PART 1: MATCHING HEADINGS OR SUMMARIES

PRACTICE EXERCISE 1

C is right. The match was cancelled because some players had heavy colds (= illness).
A is wrong as nothing suggests there will be no more future matches.
B is wrong as it seems unlikely that the match will be played this year.
D is wrong as only *most* not *all* members of the team were ill.

PRACTICE EXERCISE 2

A is right. We are told that Edinburgh is full of places of interest.
B is wrong because although some people will visit Edinburgh Castle, the articles does not say that you *must* do this.
C is wrong because we know that there are many things of interest in Edinburgh.
D is wrong because we are told that it is a problem to choose what to see in a short time.

PRACTICE EXERCISE 3

D is right. The orchestra is going away to London for the weekend.
A is wrong because the competition is not local but for orchestras from all over the country.
B is wrong because it is the orchestra's third time in the competition.
C is wrong because the orchestra has never won the competition.

PRACTICE EXERCISE 4

D is right. We are told that many hotels drop their rates (= cost less) at weekends.
A is wrong as you can stay in a top class hotel quite cheaply at the weekend.
B is wrong because we are told that *many*, not *all* hotels lower their prices at the weekend.
C is wrong as the passage does not say that business travellers never stay in hotels at the weekend.

PRACTICE EXERCISE 5

B is right. The phone proved its value by allowing the doctor to contact the emergency services.
A is wrong because the doctor was coming back from visiting a patient.
C is wrong because the doctor was a few kilometres from the farm when he was rescued.
D is wrong because the rescue services arrived in time to help the doctor.

PRACTICE EXERCISE 6

C is right. Emergency teams are trying to stop the oil polluting the river.
A is wrong because the oil has already escaped from the factory.
B is wrong because although the river looks like toffee, there is no suggestion that the oil was used for making toffees.
D is wrong as there is nothing to suggest that oil is on the banks of the river – it is the factory which is on the banks.

PRACTICE EXERCISE 7

1 E 2 B In the first paragraph we are told that the club is a place where people can talk. In the second paragraph the improved information system should make the club more efficient.
A is wrong because although writers give speeches at the club, nothing suggests that they are all members.
C is wrong as it is not stated that the club had an enthusiastic reception.
D is wrong because although requests will be dealt with better, there is no suggestion that there is a wish for more requests.
F is wrong as the writer merely *trusts* that *some* (not *all*) of their aims have been achieved.

Exam tip

Remember, in Part 1 you are looking for the main point of each paragraph.

PRACTICE EXERCISE 8

1A 2E In the first sentence we are told that the number of passengers using this service is *slightly above expectation,* which means that rather, or a few, more people are using the service. There is a possibility of more flights as Suter says that they may consider increasing frequency.

B is wrong because it is not certain that new flights will be introduced.
C is wrong because although the evening flights have done well, there may still have been some empty seats.
D is wrong because, although we are told that it is hoped more people will use this flight, the article does not say that *very few* are using the flight.
F is wrong as there are only slightly more people using the flight, not far (= a lot) more.

PRACTICE EXERCISE 9

1B 2F 3E The researchers are listening to what the staff say (= checking on their comments). The second paragraph is a set of comments which were made in the lift. In the third paragraph we learn that staff forget they are in a public place, that is a place where other people are present.

A is wrong because it is the staff not the hospital that are to blame for these comments.
C is wrong as there is no mention of a lack of communication.
D is wrong as what is said is the wrong type of thing to be saying in front of others – the language itself is not inaccurate.
G is wrong as the talking which causes problems is done in public, not in private.

PRACTICE EXERCISE 10

1 F 2 A 3 G The first hundred customers (that is, many customers) will pay only half price for their phones. In the second paragraph we learn that there will be other offers in future so that bargains will be available after the first day. In the third paragraph we learn that staff will give advice without obligation, which is to say that you will not be forced into buying a phone if you ask for advice.

B is wrong because we are told in the second paragraph that many extra items will be available.
C is wrong because only the first one hundred customers (not all the customers) will be able to buy the phones at half price.
D is wrong as there is no suggestion that visiting the shop will make phoning easier (although if you bought some of the items in the shop, they could make phoning easier).
E is wrong as there is no suggestion that phone calls will be cheaper if you buy a more expensive phone (although some of the extra items mentioned in paragraph 2 could help to make phoning cheaper).

EXAM EXERCISE 1

Music to help your brain

0 I We are told that children from schools throughout Britain took part.
1 F People's mental ability improved as they were able to work out problems.
2 A There were three groups of children, one listening to Mozart, one to a pop group and one to a discussion.
3 G The group listening to the pop group gained a mark of 56 per cent, those listening to the other programmes gained only 52 per cent.
4 C The mood of the children had changed, making them work harder, probably because they had enjoyed the music.
5 D Dr Rauscher thought that complex (=difficult) music makes the brain more active.
6 H Dr Hallam thought that adults (who took part in the experiment in California) might take in music in a different way from children (who took part in the experiment in Britain).
7 B The Minister thought that teaching in school might change as a result of this experiment.
E There is no suggestion that the children did not listen to the music by Mozart, although paragraph 4 says that they may not have been interested in this type of music.

EXAM EXERCISE 2

Making better use of time at work

0 H The paragraph is about the long hours (=time) spent working.
1 F Here we read about problems with health, families and work performance (= the bad effects of working too long both at home and at work).
2 B Employers (= those in charge) know about the problem.
3 D There are ways in which employers can help but also ways in which the individual workers can help.
4 E The people mentioned in this paragraph think that jobs are too big for them.
5 A The 'poor delegators' here feel that nobody can do a job as well as they can so they will not let other people help them.
6 G The disorganised type here does not have any system or plan for dealing with his/her work and does not finish one job before beginning the next.
C There is no suggestion that any of the types of people mentioned will not take responsibility for their work; indeed the people mentioned in paragraph 5 want to take too much responsibility.

EXAM EXERCISE 3

Railway Romances

0 I This paragraph tells us that people would normally consider railways to be unromantic places.
1 D The man was sleepy (= tired) when he got on the train, which was very full (=crowded).
2 G Although the man usually had a conversation on a train, he was so tired on this occasion that he fell asleep and could not begin to talk.
3 B The man thought the girl had left her purse on the train, which gave him a good reason for phoning her as he could tell her that he had found it.
4 F For five or six months (=often) Ron sat opposite Mary on the train.
5 C The job overseas in Australia could have been a problem but the relationship continued as Mary also went to Australia, where the two of them got married.
6 H The couple used to meet when the man had to spend a few hours waiting for a connection (= change trains) at the station.
7 A Peggy's father was angry when Jimmy brought her home late; this could have ended the relationship but, fortunately, the couple stayed together.
E In paragraph 3 we read that there was a purse left on the seat when the woman got off the train. However, the purse was not in fact hers.

EXAM EXERCISE 4

A sad ending becomes a happy ending

0 H The play did not show much promise for the future at the beginning (= unpromising start) as it closed after 26 performances and was thought to be a failure.
1 F Liliom kills himself in the play and even after his death is unable to do something good to repair all the wrong he has done. This is a tragedy.
2 A This paragraph speaks of Liliom and Molnár possibly using violence as a way of hiding their love, which they were not capable of expressing openly.
3 D Molnár finally allowed (granted permission) for Richard Rodgers and Oscar Hammerstein to base a musical on *Liliom*.
4 B Instead of the action taking place in Budapest, the musical would be set in rural America.
5 G The musical would have a happier ending than *Liliom* as the musical would end on a positive note, showing that the hero had finally done something good to help others.
6 E Richard Rodgers thought Molnár might be angry with the new ending to the play. When Molnár said that he liked the play, Rodgers was greatly relieved.
C Nobody is ashamed. In the play Liliom is not ashamed of his actions. Richard Rodgers is worried and then relieved, but not ashamed. Molnár is happy with the musical but is not ashamed of his play.

3 PART 2: MULTIPLE CHOICE

PRACTICE EXERCISE 1

1 B The word *slightly* tells us that the soldier's injuries were not serious.
2 C As the car was in collision with a lorry, we know that it must have hit another vehicle. The car was travelling on the road between Cardiff and Swansea but we do not know if it was going towards Cardiff or towards Swansea (**A**). The soldier was a passenger, not the driver (**B**).

PRACTICE EXERCISE 2

1 A As the store was going to re-open following the fire, it must have had to close down for a time. We are told that the ground floor was badly damaged but not that it was totally destroyed (**B**). The store was going to re-open on Monday; there is nothing to suggest that it would open only on Mondays (**C**).
2 C It should be pleasant to shop here as we are told that shopping here will be *an even more enjoyable experience.* We do not know if more people than before will come shopping (**A**). The word *them* must refer to the repairs; although the shopping will be enjoyable, there is no reason to think that the repairs themselves will be enjoyable (**B**).

PRACTICE EXERCISE 3

1 B The men have been arrested because the police think they stole some paintings (= works of art). The men were not caught actually stealing the paintings (**A**). The men had probably broken into houses in only two countries (England and France), not in many countries (**C**).
2 A The police are still looking for this fourth man. The police are looking for (= seeking) the man; he is not looking for the police (**B**). The man does not want to be the leader of the gang, he probably *is* the leader (**C**).

PRACTICE EXERCISE 4

1 B The fact that *frequent exercise is a way of life for many* tells us that many people are taking exercise. Although food containing fat has become less popular, this can still mean that many people are eating these foods, even though there are not so many as before (**A**). The fact that people are aware of the need for a healthy life does not mean that they are actually making the effort to live a healthier life (**C**).
2 C By being healthy, people are able to be active. Although people can begin to look younger, it is impossible for them actually to become younger (**A**). People do not lead a healthy life in order to take exercise; they take exercise in order to be healthy (**B**).

PRACTICE EXERCISE 5

1 C There were 50 runners and only 2 did not finish the race, so this means that 48 did finish the race.
2 B Peter is going to University next year so he will be carrying on studying. Although Peter plans to run when he is at University, he will not be running *to* the University – *to* means that he would be running there from his house (**A**). Peter is in his final year at school, which means that he is still studying at school although he will be leaving at the end of the year (**C**).

PRACTICE EXERCISE 6

1 B As the company's profits have dropped (= fallen) they have not made as much money this year as they did last year. However, the company has made a profit, not a loss, which makes answers **A** and **D** wrong. As the profit is less than last year's, they cannot have increased their profits (**C**).
2 D As the sales figures are disappointing, the company must have sold fewer products than they had hoped. It is true that many other companies produce computer software but this does not answer the question about the company's own new software (**A**). There is nothing to suggest that the software does not work well (**B**) or that it will be out of date by the end of the year (**C**).

PRACTICE EXERCISE 7

1 B The article mentions *tranquil dales,* which means that the countryside must be peaceful. The article mentions two towns which are nearby, which makes **A** wrong and also makes **C** wrong as the hotel cannot be lonely and isolated. All five country houses *may* possibly welcome visitors but we are not told this (**D**).

2 A The menu is more extensive in the evening, meaning that there is more choice. Hot and cold food is available both at lunchtime and in the evening, making **B** wrong. Non-residents are allowed to eat in the restaurant in the evening but there is nothing to indicate that they are not allowed to do so at lunchtime (**C**). There is nothing to indicate that the restaurant is closed in summer (**D**).

PRACTICE EXERCISE 8

1 B By worrying about the sort of world children will inherit, parents are worrying about what life is going to be like. The word *inherit* here has nothing to do with people leaving money to others when they die (**A**). The fact that the world population will grow is not given as a specific cause of worry (**C**), nor is the fact that water should be clean a specific worry (**D**).

2 D We are told that the lessons are *fun*, so they must be enjoyable. The facilities may not be used by all schools in England, only by schools in the region of the north west of England (**A**). The children learn how water gets to their homes – they do not take it home (**B**). The lessons teach children how to save (= conserve) water; they cannot actually prevent (= stop) children from wasting water (**C**).

3 A The attitude is responsible as children are being taught to face (= think about) the future. The population of the world is increasing, not falling (**B**). The fact that many children go to the facilities does not mean that North West Water has a responsible attitude (**C**), nor does providing children with a good day out necessarily show responsibility (**D**).

PRACTICE EXERCISE 9

1 C The meeting was *to promote tourism opportunities*, which means that the aim was to persuade more people to visit Scotland. The films set in Scotland would make people interested in the country – the aim was not to make people go to see these films (**A**) or to try to persuade producers to make more films of this kind (**D**). Scottish food would be available – this was just to give people an idea of what they could eat in Scotland (**B**).

2 C The *growth in tourist spending* means that visitors spent more last year. This does not necessarily mean that there were more visitors – the same number of visitors could have been spending more money (**A**). The growth was in money spent, not in salaries paid to members of the Tourist Board (**B**), nor on money spent by the Board on tourists (**D**).

3 A As *visitor numbers are expected to increase substantially,* more people are likely to come to Scotland. There is nothing to suggest that more 'scenic' films will be made here (**B**). It is expected that the films will have an effect on tourism for 15 years (**C**). Although a quarter of overseas visits are by Americans, there will also be visits by people who are not from overseas (that is, people from other parts of Britain); the proportion of Americans in the total number of visitors will be less than a quarter (**D**).

PRACTICE EXERCISE 10

1 A The man was thought to have gone walking in the mountains and had been reported missing, so it was assumed that he was lost there. The man was not an experienced mountaineer but this in itself was no reason to go looking for him (**B**), nor was the fact that he may have left the hotel in a bad temper (**D**). Earlier it had been said that the weather would be bad but we do not know if it was now going to get better (**C**).

2 A As the man was *an inexperienced mountain walker,* he could not have been used to walking in the mountains. The man had had an argument with his wife that morning – we do not know if he had many arguments with her (**B**). In the second paragraph we read that the man saw (= knew) how bad the weather was (**C**). We are told that the man did *not* think of phoning his wife (**D**).

3 D The man's wife must have been worried when he did not return to the hotel after he had gone walking in very bad weather. She did not know that he had changed his plans (**A**), nor that he had gone to Windermere (**B**), nor that he had missed a bus (**C**).

4 B The man missed the bus he had planned to catch. There is nothing to suggest that the bad weather held up the bus (**A**). The man missed the bus coming back *from* Windermere (to Keswick), not the bus going *to* Windermere (**C**). We do not know that the bus left Windermere early – the man could have arrived late for the bus (**D**).

EXAM EXERCISE 1

1 B The key words from the passage are: *wondered what type of programmes they should put on during the daytime.* It was later when they realised that they would have to entertain women as the audience would consist mainly of women (**D**).

2 D The key words from the passage are: *Knowing that the majority of the audience would be women, the broadcasters decided that the women in the serials would be strong characters.* Although most of the audience would be women, this does not mean that *no* men would listen (**B**). The passage does not state that women deal better with crises (**C**) or that men in real life have weak characters (**A**).

3 A The key words in the passage are: *these programmes always carried advertisements and, since one of the most frequently advertised products was soap...* The passage does not say that soap was the *only* thing advertised (**D**). It was the programmes which advertised soap companies, not soap companies which advertised the programmes (**B**).

4 B The key words from the passage are: *it was thought that the Americans should be shown how well the British people were standing up to the war.* The programme was not about the war itself but about how the people at home were living.

5 C The key words in the passage are: *Some people in Britain managed to hear the programme and asked for it to be broadcast for the British audience. The BBC .... finally agreed and broadcast the programme in Britain.* The passage does not tell us if the Americans liked the programme (**A**). The programme did run for six years but this was not known before the BBC decided to show the programme (**B**). The name was changed after the BBC had decided to show the programme (**D**).

6 D The key words in the passage are: *The original aim of 'The Archers' was to inform farmers of new developments in agriculture.* The other soap mentioned was about a doctor and his family (**A**). The programme is heard five evenings every week, not every evening (**B**). *The Archers* was first broadcast *in* 1951 not *before* 1951 (**C**).

7 B The key words in the passage are: *Although the series was planned to run for only thirteen weeks, it is still to be seen several nights every week.* The programme is the most popular *almost* every week, not every week (**A**). The programme was *not* shown on BBC television (**C**). It takes place *near* Manchester, not in the centre of Manchester (**D**).

8 A The key words in the passage are: *'Coronation Street' .... always contains a strong element of comedy.* There is nothing to suggest that *Coronation Street* has stronger stories (**B**). *Eastenders* is *more* realistic (**D**) and not as amusing (**C**).

EXAM EXERCISE 2

1 A The key words in the passage are: *claimed that they had built a heavier-than-air machine which they had flown.* The passage does not say that they gave *lots* of demonstrations (**B**) nor that they took the photographs themselves (**D**). It was the *Scientific American* that laughed, not the Wright brothers (**C**).

2 D The key words in the passage are: *Roosevelt ordered public trials at Fort Myers.* The trials mentioned are not court trials but tests in the open (**A**). The Wrights proved the truth of their claim, not Roosevelt (**B**). Roosevelt did not have any contact with the press in connection with this matter (**C**).

3 B The key words in the passage are: *the horse was still the principal means of transport.* Nothing suggests that horses were used only in the East (**A**) or that they were not used in Ohio (**C**). The passage says that horses were the principal (= main) means of transport *not* the only means (**D**).

4 A The key words in the passage are: *What is more surprising is that the local newspapers in their home town of Dayton, Ohio, should have ignored the Wrights*. The passage says that it is *not* surprising that intellectuals (= experts) ignored the Wrights (**B**). There is no reference to flying experiments in the East (**C**), nor to the skill of bicycle mechanics in general, only to the skill of the Wrights (**D**).

5 B The key words in the passage are: *Huffman allowed the brothers to use a large piece of farm land owned by him outside the town for their flying experiments.* Huffman allowed (= let) the Wrights use some of his land, he did not lend them money (**A**), give them land (**C**) or allow them to buy land (**D**).

6 C The key words in the passage are: *passengers wrote to the local newspapers to ask who were the young men who were regularly flying ... and why had nothing appeared about them in the papers.* People did not ask why flying was taking place (**A**). They did not know who the people were who were flying – they were not wanting to check that it was the Wrights (**B**). It was the newspapers that complained about the nuisance caused by all the letters, not people complaining about the flights (**D**).

7 D The key words in the passage are: *You mean they kept things secret by flying over an open field* – the interviewer cannot believe that this is true. The passage does not suggest that the Wrights opened any gates (**A**). It was Kumler, not the interviewer, who said that the Wrights wanted to keep the flights secret (**B**). The passage does not say that Kumler said anything to the Wrights (**C**).

8 C The passage is concerned with the newspapers' refusal to take any notice of the claims of the Wrights (that is, they refused to recognise progress (**C**). There is no suggestion that the newspapers actually tell lies (**A**), even though they do not always report everything. It was hard to convince experts and the authorities, *not* easy (**B**). The refusal to believe suggests that people will not believe anything (**D**).

EXAM EXERCISE 3

1 C The key words in the passage are: *Andrew Carnegie, the man who had provided much of the finance for its building.* The passage tells us that he gave money, but not *most* of his money (**A**). The Hall was renamed but it was not Carnegie who was responsible for the renaming (**B**). Carnegie probably did feel honoured but we are not told this, we are told that the Hall was named *in his honour* (**D**).

2 D The key words in the passage are: *a talk accompanied by slides of paintings of sunsets and landscapes, which was what the audience had been expecting.* The passage says that the audience watched the lecture with delight, which suggests that they were not frightened (**A**). People *had* been expecting to see slides (**B**). People had expected a more ordinary lecture, not a more dramatic one (**C**).

3 B The key words in the passage are: *he was aged ten.* Yehudi was wandering round the Hall instead of practising but we are not told that he did no practising at all (**A**). This was Yehudi's first appearance in the Carnegie Hall, so he could not have played here before (**C**). Although this was Yehudi's first appearance at the Carnegie Hall the passage does not tell us that he had never appeared on a stage before (**D**).

4 B The guard had frightened the young boy by telling him about musicians having their head cut off when they did not play well. As this made him rush back to practise, it suggests that he believed what the guard had told him (**B**). There is nothing in the passage to suggest that Yehudi realised that he needed to practise (**A**) or that the guard was about to attack him (**C**). He had already asked what the axe was for (**D**).

5 A The pianist had got lost in the music, not in New York – he knew which building he was in. The pianist was telling the truth as they were in the Carnegie Hall but he was not giving the information that the violinist needed (**B**). The violinist had lost his *place* in the music (= he did not know which part he should be playing), he had not lost the sheet of music itself (**C**). The pianist did know where they were (in the Carnegie Hall) (**D**).

6 D The key words in the passage are: *On the day of the concert, cars came to a halt all over the city*. The passage tells us that nobody was seriously injured, which means that **A** is not correct; similarly **C** suggests, wrongly, that many people were injured in the Hall. There were crowds surrounding the Carnegie Hall, not in all parts of New York (**B**).

7 C The key words in the passage are: *In the 1950s the building was threatened with demolition*. Isaac Stern led the campaign against demolition – it was not just he alone who stopped the demolition (**A**). The Hall was sold to the City of New York in 1960, not in 1950 (**B**). The campaign was *against* the demolition of the Hall (**D**).

8 D The key words in the passage are: *Over the years the most famous musicians, singers and entertainers in the world have appeared there – no doubt they will continue to do so for many years to come*. It is true that the greatest entertainers have appeared in the Hall but this tells us nothing about the future, which is what the question asks about (**A**). The passage suggests that the Hall will still be successful in the future (**B**). The Hall has already been named as a national landmark (**C**).

EXAM EXERCISE 4

1 D The key words are *I never saw much of him*, when speaking of Father. We are told that *seeing his father* did not worry *the child*, not that *the child* did not worry *the father* (**A**). It is not true that the child *never* saw his father; he did not see much of him, so he must have seen a little of him (**B**). There is no suggestion that the child annoyed his father (**C**).

2 B The key words are *an uncomfortable squeeze between Mother and him,* suggesting that the bed was not big enough for all three. The *squeeze* was because of three being in the bed, not because mother was squeezing the child (**A**). We are not told that it was unusual for the child to be in the bed so early (**C**). The child found the smell of smoke *pleasant* so this could not have made him uncomfortable (**D**).

3 D Father thought the souvenirs might be handy (= useful). Father put the souvenirs on top of the wardrobe, not inside it (**A**). Although the child describes the souvenirs as treasures, they do not seem to be very valuable things (**B**). Mother did not seem to value the souvenirs but this would not be a reason for keeping them (**C**).

4 A The key words are *ready to shine and rejoice* and *Life seemed....full of possibilities*. Life seemed simple, the child was not simple (**B**). The child felt that life held possibilities, not that life was possible (as he was obviously alive) (**C**). The child was happy, not funny (= amusing) (**D**).

5 B The key words are *I began to tell her of my schemes* (= plans). Mother went to make breakfast later (**A**). Mother did not ask about his schemes, he told her about them (**C**). He did go to sleep in the bed but it was not as soon as he got in (**D**).

6 D The key words are *we could not afford one until father came back*. Although Father was away at war, the war was not the reason for not having a baby (**A**). There were babies in the street but there is no suggestion that there were too many (**B**). Although mother said that they could not afford a baby, this was not the problem as the passage suggests that they would be able to have one when Father came back (**C**).

7 A The key words are *it was probably a cheap baby* (that is, not a good quality one). The child says that the price could not have been too high because even the poor Geneys could afford one (**B**). The fact that the Geneys were poor would not have made the mother not want the baby (**C**). As the passage suggests that the Geneys' baby was a cheap one, the baby could not have been too good for Mother (**D**).

Exam tip

In Part 2, remember to read the question and the 4 answers very carefully. Only one of the answers is right – the others may be designed to mislead you!

4 PART 3: GAPPED TEXT

PRACTICE EXERCISE 1

D B C A

Sentence **D** tells us what is the main point of this story – notice that the sentence mentions *a large amount of jewellery* and *a house*. Sentence **B** links to **D** by the words *the house*. Sentence **C** is linked to **B** by the words *in this way,* referring to the way in which the thieves entered the house. Sentence **A** finishes the story by referring to a situation which has already been mentioned (leaving a window open). (It is almost possible for **A** to be the first sentence but the paragraph would need to have some phrase such as *the reason for this is that* to link it to the next sentence, **D**.)

PRACTICE EXERCISE 2

B D A C

Sentence **B** sets the scene by telling us the basic details of what happened (notice the use of *a* in front of *dangerous situation)*. Sentence **D** begins to tell us more about the situation; again *a* is used in front of *horse* as this is the first time that the horse has been mentioned. Sentence **A** is linked to **D** by *the horse* and we are told more about what the horse did. Sentence **A** has told us that the horse ran down the road, **C** now tells us what happened when it ran down the road.

PRACTICE EXERCISE 3

B D C E A

Sentence **B** gives us the main theme of the passage. Sentence **D** is linked to **B** by *This* referring to *the increase in sales*. Sentence **C** now tells us a little more about the campaign which is mentioned in **D**. As **C** has told us about the form of the campaign, sentence **E** goes on to say why this type of campaign is successful. Sentence **A** finally deals with the effect that the campaign has had on other advertisers.

PRACTICE EXERCISE 4

D A C E B

Sentence **D** sets the scene and gives us the full name of the winner of the competition. Sentence **A** is linked to **D** by *Jane's story*; we know that Jane had written a story, we are now told what the story was about. Sentence **C** gives us some more information about this story. Sentence **E** now moves on to talking about the prize money. Sentence **B** is linked to **E** by *the money* and tells us a little more about Jane's reaction to winning the money.

PRACTICE EXERCISE 5

B In **B** we are told that the lights were stuck on red, which means that they failed to work. Sentence **A** is not correct as it states that there were only two or three vehicles on the road although the passage says that the junction was busy and that a large queue had built up. Sentence **C** is incorrect as it is clear that the situation was not brought under control until the police arrived after ten minutes. Sentence **D** is wrong as the problem was that the traffic lights were not working – this was not an extra problem as suggested in **D**.

PRACTICE EXERCISE 6

C There has been a change in opening hours, which should be more convenient for customers, thus, the supermarket is *responding to customer demand* (**C**). Sentence **A** is wrong because if it were thought that the staff were already working long enough, the opening hours of the supermarket would probably not have been made greater. Sentence **B** is wrong because if customers found the old opening hours satisfactory, there would be no point in changing them. Sentence **D** is wrong because if few people wanted to shop after working, there would be no point in allowing the shop to stay open later (**D**).

PRACTICE EXERCISE 7

A Sentence **B** is wrong as the factory has not yet been pulled down. Sentence **C** is wrong as the factory is to be pulled down (= demolished), not to be re-opened. Sentence **D** is wrong as it is stated that the factory will be pulled down and that it is thought that the factory has already been bought.

PRACTICE EXERCISE 8

D Sentence **A** is wrong as we learn that the postman was not able to return home for several days and was thus not able to continue delivering his letters that day. Sentence **B** is wrong as it does not really link with the following sentence; the word *he* suggests that it was the young man who was making good progress. Sentence **C** is wrong because if the man was not able to return home for several days, he must have been taken to hospital.

PRACTICE EXERCISE 9

1D This follows on from the announcement of Mrs Wilson's retirement by telling us how long she had worked in the school.

2A The key word here is *them,* which must refer to changes which are mentioned in the sentence before and in the following sentence.

3C The previous sentence has told us that Mrs Wilson is looking forward to retirement. We are now told of something she intends to do. The sentence also fits in neatly with the following sentence, which has the key words *Apart from* ***this.***

Sentence B cannot fill any of the gaps. As Mrs Wilson has retired from teaching, this means that she has stopped teaching and will not be taking on a new job as a teacher.

Exam tip

1 When you have to put missing sentences into paragraphs (as in Exam Exercises 1-3), make sure you read the whole paragraph before choosing. There could be clues in what comes before the missing sentence and what comes after it.

2 When you are dealing with missing paragraphs (as in Exam Exercise 4), read the paragraph that comes after a gap as well as the one that comes before. Again, there could be clues in both.

3 When you have decided where all the missing sentences or paragraphs go, try and give yourself time to read through the whole passage again, incorporating the missing sentences or paragraphs. This is a good way of checking whether it all makes sense.

EXAM EXERCISE 1

Qantas

0E The first paragraph deals with a few general facts about the airline. Sentence **E** does the same.

1C This paragraph has been about the failure to enter the race which is mentioned in sentence **C**. The word *However* acts as a key word linking this sentence to the failure mentioned in the paragraph.

2I The paragraph speaks of the difficulty of travelling by car in this part of the country. The key words *on the journey* link this sentence about the difficulties of travelling with the paragraph.

3H The paragraph speaks of the two men being given money to start their project for air travel. The sentence continues the theme by speaking of their first planes.

4D The key word here is *patients* as the paragraph has been about setting up a flying doctor service to help the sick in remote parts of the country.

5G This paragraph has been concerned with the expansion of the airline's services. Mention is made of flights carrying mail and now sentence **G** brings in the idea of carrying passengers abroad for the first time. (It could be tempting to think that **A** would be the most appropriate sentence here but as no mention has so far been made of overseas passenger flights, one cannot speak of *more overseas passenger services.*)

6A An overseas passenger service (Sydney to London) has just been mentioned, so it is reasonable to continue by speaking of *more overseas passenger services*. (See note above on answer 5.)

7 F The paragraph has just spoken of Qantas and Australian becoming one; the sentence goes on to speak of the two airlines joining together.

Sentence B does not fit in any gap; it is completely the opposite of what is stated in the last paragraph.

EXAM EXERCISE 2

Police to use buses

0G The first paragraph tells us that the police will be travelling by bus and this sentence explains how this will happen.

1A The key words are *sit here*, which refer to *sit on the top deck*.

2E The word *Howeve*r links the sentence to the sentence before, but the main link here is with the following sentence, where the police inspector shows how the police will be treated like the rest of the public.

3C The key word is *Howeve*r in the following sentence in the paragraph. The mention of buses not being used for emergency calls is contrasted in the following sentence with the use of buses for non-urgent calls.

4H The paragraph has just spoken about a reduction in spending; this sentence shows how the scheme will lead to less expense.

5F The key word is *us*. A policewoman is speaking in this paragraph and saying that she thinks the scheme is a good idea; the sentence continues the theme of this being a good idea.

6B The key words are ***our** bus drivers,* as the person speaking in this paragraph is the manager of the local bus company.

Sentence D cannot be correct as it speaks of this scheme as having been successful in the past, but this is impossible as it has not begun yet.

EXAM EXERCISE 3

Looking for work

0B The boy had left school and so was hoping to find a job.

1H The key words are *these questions,* referring to the questions which were asked at the Labour Exchange when a young person was looking for a job.

2D The key words are *attended* and *the card*. The paragraph speaks of people being given a card to take to a firm where a job was available.

3F The writer speaks of failing to find jobs with the help of the Labour Exchange and now mentions that he also looked for work by looking at the job advertisements in the papers.

4A The *he* refers to the boy's uncle. The uncle is mentioned in this paragraph in connection with the boy's search for work.

5I Again *he* refers to the boy's uncle. A key word is *there*. We are told that the uncle accepted a job he was offered and this leads on to our learning how long he remained in the job.

6G The link with the paragraph is *Mr Brownson*. We have been told about two shops and then in this sentence there is the possibility of a job in Mr Brownson's shop.

7E The key words are *run after the other boy* as these link with the paragraph which tells us that this other boy had left the shop and was going to the wrong place.

Sentence C is wrong. In this sentence *he* could refer to the writer, the writer's uncle or the boy who went to the wrong shop. It must be untrue as we know that the writer had not found a job since leaving school. The same was probably true of the other boy. The boy's uncle had been out of work for almost a year. However, as he was over 30, this suggests that he had worked for more than six months immediately after leaving school.

Horse racing

EXAM EXERCISE 4

0D This follows on from the opening paragraph, giving a general introduction to horse racing.

1C The key words are *jump racing* and *flat racing*. The two types of racing have been mentioned in the previous paragraph; this paragraph now tells us a little more about the two types of racing.

2G The key words here are *In spite of this*. The previous paragraph has stated that flat racing is considered to be superior but this paragraph informs us that the most famous race is a jump race.

3E The previous paragraph has spoken of the dangers in horse racing thus making the link with **E** through the key words *Even though jockeys are well aware of the dangers*.

4B The previous paragraph is about the fact that jockeys do not earn much money. This paragraph continues with the theme of jockeys needing the money they earn from riding.

5H The key words linking this with the previous paragraph are *She*, *fell badly*, *Gee*, *hospital where she stayed for the next month*. All these words link to the previous paragraph, which mentions this female rider's fall and her having to stay in hospital.

6F The previous paragraph was about Gee's determination to ride again in spite of the lack of enthusiasm from her friends and family; this paragraph gives us some information as to why she wants to ride.

Paragraph A does not fit in any of the gaps. It says that jockeys do not bother about making money as they love riding so much. However, in the passage we read that although jockeys do love riding, they also need the money which they earn.

5 PART 4: MULTIPLE MATCHING

Words in italics are taken directly from the passages. Sometimes an answer is explained simply by showing the words from the passage which answer the question.

PRACTICE EXERCISE 1

1 C This would be suitable as it would be a view of the sea from the coast.
2 E This would be suitable as it would contain buildings (= examples of architecture).
3 A There would be plenty of action in a picture of a battle.
4 D A stream and a hill would almost certainly be in the countryside.
5 B There would be a display of clothes at a fashion show.

PRACTICE EXERCISE 2

1 Train The last flight leaves at 6.00 p.m., the last train does not leave until 7.30 p.m..
2 Air The first flight arrives at 8.30 a.m., the first train does not arrive until 10.30 a.m..
3 Train The train costs £45, the air fare £120.
4 Train There are no flights in the afternoon, there are train services throughout the day.
5 Air The flight takes only one hour, the train takes four hours.

PRACTICE EXERCISE 3

1 B **B** tells us it was Meadow Hill Hospital, **A** says simply 'a hospital'.
2 B **B** tells us the jobs of both people. **A** tells us the job of only the motor cyclist.
3 A **A** tells us that the accident happened in front of Melton Town Hall, **B** simply that it happened in Melton
4 A **A** tells us *they were treated for shock*. **B** says nothing about their treatment.
5 B **B** tells us that *the road was very wet*; **A** says nothing about the road conditions.

PRACTICE EXERCISE 4

1 B **B** tells us that the centre will be open *within the next two months.*
2 A **A** tells us about the activities (*discos, indoor games, speakers, excursions, etc.*).
3 A Both articles tell us that the centre will be open from 7.00 p.m. four nights a week, but article **A** goes on to tell us which nights these will be.
4 B **B** tells us that young people complain there is nothing to do in the town, thus suggesting that the young people need a youth centre.
5 A **A** mentions an upper age limit of 21; **B** mentions simply people aged over 16.

PRACTICE EXERCISE 5

1 Patience We are told that *in the end all is well*, that is, the ending is happy.
2 Talents The play is historical as it deals with a true story from the past.
3 Arrest This is a fast-moving play as it contains *plenty of action.*
4 Patience This is a *love story* and, therefore, romantic.
5 Arrest As this is a *highly amusing* play, it must be funny.

PRACTICE EXERCISE 6

1 Dooleys Dooleys serve lunch as they are open from 11 o'clock in the morning.
2 Crawfords There is a *live band* providing music on Fridays and Saturdays.
3 Dooleys Dooleys say you can call in for *just a drink.*
4 Beltons There is much description of Beltons restaurant but little about the food.
5 Crawfords The speciality is based on two fish, – *sole and salmon.*

PRACTICE EXERCISE 7

1 This Week The magazine deals with *stock markets* and *investment* (= finance).
2 Weekly Post Half the magazine is about sport, so it will contain cricket reports.
3 This Week There are stories from abroad, that is to say, from other countries.
4 Weekly Post Half of this magazine is designed to make people laugh.
5 Weekly Review The magazine contains stories about famous people.

PRACTICE EXERCISE 8

1 B Thomas Stanley did a lot of *hard work* raising money for the block.
2 C Science lessons have been in classrooms or at a nearby school.
3 A **A** and **C** tell us there are 12 laboratories but **A** also tells us the subjects to be taught there.
4 C Article **C** tells us that the professor said young people need to know science.
5 A Article **A** says staff (= teachers) *are looking forward to working* in the centre.

PRACTICE EXERCISE 9

1 Jane The girl likes animals and Jane has a dog and lives on a farm where there will probably be animals. The girl likes languages and Jane likes French. (Sally has a dog and cat but we do not know if she likes languages.)
2 Tim Tim has travelled abroad and likes camping and walking – both outdoor activities.
3 Peter Peter is a boy and (last sentence) clearly likes going out.
4 Tim Tim likes Physics and Chemistry (science subjects) and walking in the country.
5 Sally The girl likes children so she will enjoy being with Sally's younger brothers and sisters. She will also be able to go to the shops in Bristol with Sally.

PRACTICE EXERCISE 10

1 Edinburgh Edinburgh Airport is 11 miles from the city centre.
2 Birmingham Here they will have *a quick ...... journey through the terminal.*
3 Manchester Terminals 1 and 2 are mentioned.
4 Glasgow *International passengers* (= coming from abroad) *arrive at ground floor level, passengers on internal flights arrive at first floor level.*
5 Manchester We are told there is a *free bus service* between the terminals.

Exam tip

Remember, in Part 4 you are looking for specific details, so you need to concentrate to find the differences between passages that may seem quite similar.

EXAM EXERCISE 1

0 E The flat has only one bedroom, which is suitable for a single woman, and is near the airport and motorway, which will be convenient for travelling.

1 D This property is suitable as the house is not too big and is fairly close to the park and fields, where the dogs can be exercised. A flat (such as **E**) would not be a good place to keep two dogs.

2 F This house would be suitable as the couple could work on repairing it. It is also close to a school for their son.

3 C This would seem to be a fairly cheap flat suitable for a student. The fact that it is opposite the railway station would mean that he could travel home quite easily.

4 B This well-off (= having plenty of money) family could afford this magnificent house. There would be enough room for their children and their cars.

5 G The two nurses would need two separate bedrooms. As the nurses do not have a car, it would be useful to be near the bus station.

6 A The house is big enough for the family and convenient for the children's school. Property **F** would not be suitable as it is some distance from the city.

7 H This cottage in a quiet country village would suit people wanting a peaceful life.

8 I A rich widow would be able to afford a luxury flat. This one is in the city centre, where she likes to be, and has a lift and a room for friends to stay in.

9 E A pilot should be able to afford a luxury flat. As he or she is unmarried, one bedroom would be sufficient. It is useful that the airport is nearby.

10 B As this family is wealthy and as they would want to impress guests who visit them on business, this magnificent house would suit them.

11 H As the couple work from home, they would not need to be in the city. The fact that the cottage is in a country village would allow them to go on long country walks. (Property **D** would not be so suitable as they would probably not be able to go on such long walks in the park and the fields. Property **B** would be too big for just a couple.)

12 & 13 A & D in any order These are the only two properties which have gardens and are not in the countryside.

14 B As the flat is on two levels (or floors) it would be necessary to go up stairs.

15 A The structure of the house is safe but the inside does need to have some work done on it to bring it up to date. This is why it is being offered at a reasonable price.

EXAM EXERCISE 2

0 D People in this job have to work in all *parts of the country*. (Job **H** does not fit the description as the travelling is only local – in *a small geographical area*.)

1 H You will have to call at *customers' homes* to collect or deliver parcels.

2 B In this job you work *from mid-July until the end of October* (only a few months).

3 E The salary you will earn will depend *upon age and experience*.

4 F People who apply for this job *must have a knowledge of at least one foreign language*. (For job **B** it is *useful but is **not** essential* to know a foreign language.)

5 H In this job you have to *work on your own* – that is, *alone*.

6 G In this job you will have to deal with *incoming and outgoing mail* (= post).

7 C You will be with old people in this job as you have to *care for elderly people*.

8 G In this job you have to work *from 2.00 p.m. to 8.00 p.m.* (part of the afternoon and evening.)

9 A In this job you will *spend two years ..... learning all aspects of supermarket work*. This time is referred to as *this period of training*. (In job **F**, although there is two years of training abroad, the whole of the training programme lasts 3 years.)

10 & 11 E & G in any order In **E** applicants must be *smart in appearance*. In **G** candidates must be *extremely smart*.

12 & 13 D & H in any order In **D** we are told that a *current driving licence is essential* (that is to say, you must be able to drive). In **H** the applicant must be able to drive a car or van in order to collect and deliver the parcels.

14 & 15 B & F in any order In **B** representatives will have to work *in various European countries*. In **F** we read that training will be in a *variety of different countries*.

EXAM EXERCISE 3

0 C On this holiday you can go on gentle walks in the countryside or go for journeys in the car.

1 F On this holiday the couple would have a break and be able to earn some money at the same time.

2 B This holiday would be suitable for the family as families with young children are given a particularly warm welcome. The children would like the beach being nearby.

3 G The man would enjoy this holiday as there are theatres nearby. As he has plenty of money, he would be able to stay in this hotel.

4 B This guest house is at the seaside and is not too expensive.

5 D This holiday will provide hard walking as it is in the mountains. As the girl is independent minded, she will not be bothered about there being no excursions led by a guide from the lodge.

6 F This holiday is cheap and is different from normal holidays as there is work to do which should stop the man from getting bored.

7 C As this is a self-catering holiday, the men can have their meals at any time they like. It is also possible to go fishing in a river nearby.

8 E This holiday is in a very comfortable hotel and there is dancing every night. (Holiday **G** is also in a comfortable hotel but there is no mention of dancing.)

9 H There are plenty of activities organised here and the club is in the countryside.

10 & 11 E & G in any order Both of these holidays are in expensive hotels which mention their excellent accommodation and meals.

12 & 13 A & H in any order Both of these holidays offer plenty of activities.

14 B Holidays **A**, **B** and **E** are all at the seaside.

15 D Hills are mentioned in both descriptions. No activities are organised on holiday **C**. There is no mention of villages in holiday **H**. Although rooms are for two people on holiday **H**, there is no mention of the size of rooms on holiday **C**.

EXAM EXERCISE 4

0 C In **C** William Blake goes *to the west to take up a job*.

1 D In **D** the film is about some Americans *whose lives are based totally on work*.

2 G The film takes place *within a single eventful night* (that is less than 24 hours).

3 B The visitors impose *their London ways on the rural inhabitants*.

4 A The film *owes its charm to ..... a magnificent performance by Liv Tyler*.

5 F The young woman Finn *is introduced to a group of elderly ladies* with whom she then spends much of her time listening to their stories.

6 H This film *was based on a stage play*.

7 C In **C** the changes in Blake's circumstances *lead this law-abiding citizen into crime*.

8 G In this film *the guests also begin to reveal their own secrets and desires*.

9 E This film would be *unremarkable* but for the fact that *it makes good use of its beautiful Italian locations*.

10 B Ieuan and Michael Lloyd are both in love with Helen, the professor's wife.

11 H This film was one of the *comedies of the 1940s*, that is over 40 years ago.

12 & 13 C & D in any order There is no mention of love in either of these films.

14 & 15 A & E in any order In **A** Lucy goes from the USA to Italy after the death of her mother, in **E** Miss Bentley travels to Italy after the death of her father.

TRIAL PAPER A

Problem for students

PART 1

0 H In this paragraph we read that students have not had any hot water for a week.

1 B In this paragraph we read about what students have done (= how they have reacted to the problem of no water).

2 E One student says that it is impossible to wash, showing that it is impossible to keep clean.

3 A In spite of the complaints, the university does not seem to be showing interest (= there is no concern from the university).

4 C The extra facilities such as showers are no use without water.

5 F There does not seem to be much chance of 64 students finding new accommodation.

6 D The students seem to be suggesting that the problem is worse than it is (= exaggerating) as not all the flats are without water and work is being done on those which are without water.

G According to the last paragraph all flats now have water so one cannot say that the water will be restored (= will be available) in the future.

The Irish language today

PART 2

7 D The key words in the passage are: *Until about the seventeenth century, Irish was the normal everyday language of Ireland.* Many people left the country in the nineteenth century, not the seventeenth (**A**). Official business was in English later in the century (**B**). Although the English began to impose their language in the seventeenth century, nothing suggests that the English began invading only in that century (**C**).

8 C The key words in the passage are: *This practical motivation to use English grew even stronger when people began to leave Ireland.* The end of the paragraph tells us that knowing only Irish would be a problem (**A**). There is nothing to suggest that life would be easy in an English-speaking country (**B**). Although the people would need to know English, there is no suggestion that they should pretend not to be Irish (**D**).

9 D The key words in the passage are: *Even in the areas of the country which are supposed to be Irish-speaking, the use of the language is decreasing. These areas, known officially as the 'Gaeltacht'...* 83,000 people live in the Gaeltacht but they do not all use Irish as the normal language of communication (**A**). Of the 83,000 people, only 30,000 use it as a first language – this is not *almost everybody* (**B**). Almost all of the 83,000 people understand Irish – 30,000 use it as their first language (**C**).

10 A The key words in the passage are: *Until 1973 pupils had to gain a pass in Irish if they were to be awarded their school leaving certificate. This rule was very unpopular and was dropped.* All pupils have to learn Irish, which makes **B** and **D** wrong. Pupils had to pass Irish *until* 1973, but *since then* have not needed to do so (**C**).

11 C The key words in the passage are: *French or German, which can at least be useful for getting a job.* French and German do not actually make sure (= ensure) that pupils can get a job (**A**). Pupils may find French and German useful but we do not know if they think the subjects are boring (**B**). There is examination pressure in secondary schools but this is not made easier by doing French and German (**D**).

12 B The key words in the passage are: *a scheme .... that has grown up in response to the demands of parents.* The schools do have better results and the teachers are more committed (= motivated) but this could not have been known before the schools were built (**A** & **D**). It is in the towns where these schools are found and it was mentioned in the paragraph above that all pupils learn Irish (**C**).

13 A The key words in the passage are: *One criticism made of these schools is that they could be distracting pupils from learning 'more useful' modern languages*. Classes are small and examination results are above average, but these make the schools popular with parents and do not lead to criticism (**B** & **C**). There is some criticism about possible problems with more useful languages but there is no suggestion that everything taught is of no use (**D**).

14 B The key words in the passage are: *The most surprising development of recent years has been the rapid rise in the number of state schools in towns that do all their main teaching in Irish*. This suggests that the end of the Irish language is not in sight yet (**A**) and that the language is not dead (**C**). However, its use is apparently decreasing in the villages (even in the Gaeltacht) (**D**).

PART 3

Blackpool

0 C The link here is with the following sentence. Sentence **C** mentions seaside resorts and the sentence following the gap in the paragraph makes reference to *the biggest of these resorts*.

15 H The reference to the *industrial towns* here links up with mention in the paragraph of towns which were *smoke-filled*. In the following sentence a key word is *This,* referring to the arrival of the railways.

16 A The fact that visitors wanted entertainment links up with mention of *theatres* and *dance halls*. Discussion of Blackpool Tower is continued in the second part of the paragraph.

17 F A second tower has just been mentioned in the passage. This sentence tells us something about this tower.

18 G The key word here is *trams*. There has just been a reference to trams in the passage. In the following sentence we are told that trams have been re-introduced in several cities.

19 B Mention has just been made in this paragraph of Blackpool having the longest holiday season and then this sentence goes on to speak about how the town is kept busy throughout the year.

20 E The passage has just stated that not everyone likes Blackpool (Blackpool *is not to everyone's taste)* and sentence **E** suggests at the beginning why some people (those who like *smart sophisticated* places) would not like Blackpool.

Sentence D does not fit in any of the gaps. It might be tempting to think that it would fit in gap 17 but the reference in that paragraph is to the second Blackpool tower, not the first.

PART 4

0 E Pupils here have to study two foreign languages and examination results in languages are good.

21 B This is a small school where the main aim of the school is to care for its pupils – this should suit a shy and quiet boy. The school also does well in Art, which is good for a boy who likes painting.

22 D This school does not place too much emphasis on academic success, so this should suit a girl who is not very clever. As all pupils have to learn a musical instrument, this girl should be able to learn to play the flute.

23 A Science seems to be very important at this school, as is music. This boy should be able to sing in the choir.

24 G At this school the girl will be able to help people as the school *organises various activities for old people*. She will like the school because sport is important there.

25 C The school is suitable for a boy liking animals as there are hens, pigs and sheep here.

26 G This school is suitable for a girl wanting to be an actress as it has its own theatre and puts on several productions every year. In addition, all pupils have drama lessons in the first three years.

27 F Sport is important in this school and many pupils go on to university.

28 & 29 A & E in any order Both these schools have good examination results in science.

30 & 31 A & C in any order Music and travel feature in both these schools. School **A** has *a strong musical tradition* and the orchestra went on a tour of Germany last year. Music is important in school **C** and the school organises many trips abroad.

32 & 33 D & G in any order These two schools are *not* in the centre of town. Schools **B** and **C** are also away from the centre of town but are for boys only.

34 A Only one school refers to the clothes pupils should wear; this is school **E**, which says that pupils must *adhere to the school's dress code*, that is to say they must follow school rules about the clothes they wear.

35 C Both schools accept boys. Neither school is near the town centre (**A**). The schools are not the same size – one has 400 pupils, the other 750 (**B**). Neither school seems to stress academic standards too greatly (**D**).

TRIAL PAPER B

Cookery course

PART 1

0 H As we are told that the daily schedule was more like that of a work camp than that of a leisure break, the course was clearly not intended for people wanting a holiday.

1 C The word *amateur* shows that none of the cooks could be professional.

2 E The third sentence of this paragraph describes each day's theme.

3 D As the kitchen staff work long hours and as the work is exhausting, work must be hard for the staff.

4 A Students are told that the aim of the course is to show *you how we do it here*.

5 F We read that the students enjoyed finding out about the other people on the course.

6 B One *element* (or part) of the meal was something we had prepared ourselves (= *the product of our own labours*).

G Although there were meals every evening, we are not told that they were huge or accompanied by champagne. The only meal that was huge and with champagne was on the final evening (last paragraph).

Going to the library in the past

PART 2

7 B The key words are *variety....of books*; there seem to be many more books to choose from now; the writer had far less choice. In spite of the variety of books, the passage does not say that children always get what they want (**A**). Although children look through a lot of books, there is no suggestion that they behave badly (**C**). The passage does not tell us if children spend more time reading books (**D**).

8 D The key words are *They were kept in some remote corner of the building to which only the librarian had access*. There was a list of authors in the catalogues *(in alphabetical order)* (**A**). The children were not able to look at the illustrations, so it was impossible to know if they would be interesting or not (**B**). There is no suggestion that there were only a few book titles, but that the children *knew very few authors by name, and even fewer book titles* (**C**).

9 C The writer speaks of catalogues which he had to use to find which books were available. It was necessary to write out a list *after* one had found out what was available (**A**). Children had to look at the catalogues rather than ask the librarian (**B**). The list was one's order but one did not write this until one knew what was available (**D**).

10 D The key words are *titles often gave little guidance as to what the book was about.* Although the children knew few book titles, this does not mean that they did not know any at all (**A**). The fact that the titles gave little guidance means that they did *not* tell the writer what they were about (**B**). We do not know if there were many titles or not (**C**).

11 C The key words are *The librarian did not allow us to bring back any book until we had kept it for at least a week.* You had to keep a book for at least a week, not just till the following day, even though you may have wanted to return it then (**A**) (**D**). You could not return a book in less than (= within) a week, you had to keep it for a week or more (**B**).

12 A The key words are *Your hands were inspected.* The librarian sent only the children who had dirty hands to wash them, not all the children (**B**). She told some children to wash their hands but did not wash them for the children (**C**). She looked at their hands, she did not ask them if they were dirty (**D**).

13 B The key words are *we never got blamed for something we had not done.* The librarian would be able to find out *if* a book had been damaged, not *why* it had been damaged (**A**). As you were returning the book, it would be too late to find out if somebody else had damaged the book previously (**C**). If you had damaged a book, this would be found out and you *would* be blamed (**D**).

14 A The key words are *They led me into the land of story, romance and adventure.* The librarian gave him access to books, she did not tell him stories (**B**). The books, not the librarian, helped cheer him up (**C**). The passage does not suggest that she made him feel like an adult (**D**).

PART 3

A lucky passenger

0 G The first paragraph has introduced us to the situation. This paragraph tells us more about the scene on the runway.

15 C We have been told in the previous paragraph that the passenger had landed at terminal four. This paragraph continues the story as she goes to terminal one.

16 F We know that a search has begun and in the next paragraph learn that the flight leaves its stand. This must, therefore, be the time when the passenger is taken to get on the plane.

17 D We have learnt in the previous paragraph that the plane has left its stand and so by now it would be some distance from the terminal waiting to take off.

18 A The customer-service agent is rushing across the runways by car in order to reach the plane so it is to be expected that there would be radio conversation between the agent (Mr Hughes), the traffic controllers and the pilot (Captain Swift).

19 H We can assume that the car carrying the glasses has reached the plane and we are told that the captain has got some string. The next event would be for the glasses to be pulled onto the plane.

20 B The previous paragraph has told us that many of the passengers watched what was happening so it is reasonable that the remark about Ms Schwartz not watching should follow this.

Sentence E does not fit into the passage. The glasses could not possibly have been pulled onto the plane after it had taken off and was flying. Also the whole of the passage has been telling us that it was the captain (or pilot) who actually managed to get the glasses onto the plane, not two passengers.

0 G We are told that *Upper Street......will be closed to traffic for the final day.*

21 C This entertainment seems dangerous as the performers will be *10 metres above the audience's heads, and without safety nets.*

22 A This entertainment consists of a *mobile* (= can be moved) *theatre* which can be *erected in sports and leisure centres around the country.*

23 I We are told that the man's anger *subsides* (= disappears) when his wife's numbers win the lottery.

24 E Bryson is looking for *the perfect American small town* but does not manage to find any such thing.

25 F In this entertainment *an astronaut is trapped in orbit around the earth*, that is to say, he is in space going round the earth.

26 B Jackson Browne will be *performing songs from his latest album*, that is to say songs that he has recently recorded.

27 H This entertainment contains *a break-neck steam train ride*, that is to say, a very fast journey.

28 I This entertainment is *about the effects on a family of becoming overnight millionaires.*

29 G A group is coming to this festival *with giant wooden camels.*

30 H This entertainment is about the life of Isambard Kingdom Brunel, who lived in the 19th century, that is over a hundred years ago.

31 E Bryson has memories of *the films of his youth and childhood holidays.*

32 & 33 **D & H in any order** In **D** the play in York is a children's opera. In **H** the story is told *through the eyes of a child* and is *suitable for anyone over six years of age.*

34 & 35 **C & F in any order** In C the show is based on *the themes of solitude* (= loneliness) *and fear.* In **F** the performers try to *find a cure for loneliness.*

UNIVERSITY *of* CAMBRIDGE
Local Examinations Syndicate

SAMPLE

[redacted]

For Supervisor's use only

Shade here if the candidate is ABSENT or has WITHDRAWN

Examination Details	9999/01 99/D99
Examination Title	First Certificate in English
Centre/Candidate No.	AA999/9999
Candidate Name	A.N. EXAMPLE

• Sign here if the details above are correct

X

• Tell the Supervisor now if the details above are not correct

Candidate Answer Sheet: FCE Paper 1 Reading

Use a pencil

Mark ONE letter for each question.

For example, if you think **B** is the right answer to the question, mark your answer sheet like this:

Change your answer like this:

1	A	B	C	D	E	F	G	H	I
2	A	B	C	D	E	F	G	H	I
3	A	B	C	D	E	F	G	H	I
4	A	B	C	D	E	F	G	H	I
5	A	B	C	D	E	F	G	H	I
6	A	B	C	D	E	F	G	H	I
7	A	B	C	D	E	F	G	H	I
8	A	B	C	D	E	F	G	H	I
9	A	B	C	D	E	F	G	H	I
10	A	B	C	D	E	F	G	H	I
11	A	B	C	D	E	F	G	H	I
12	A	B	C	D	E	F	G	H	I
13	A	B	C	D	E	F	G	H	I
14	A	B	C	D	E	F	G	H	I
15	A	B	C	D	E	F	G	H	I
16	A	B	C	D	E	F	G	H	I
17	A	B	C	D	E	F	G	H	I
18	A	B	C	D	E	F	G	H	I
19	A	B	C	D	E	F	G	H	I
20	A	B	C	D	E	F	G	H	I
21	A	B	C	D	E	F	G	H	I
22	A	B	C	D	E	F	G	H	I
23	A	B	C	D	E	F	G	H	I
24	A	B	C	D	E	F	G	H	I
25	A	B	C	D	E	F	G	H	I
26	A	B	C	D	E	F	G	H	I
27	A	B	C	D	E	F	G	H	I
28	A	B	C	D	E	F	G	H	I
29	A	B	C	D	E	F	G	H	I
30	A	B	C	D	E	F	G	H	I
31	A	B	C	D	E	F	G	H	I
32	A	B	C	D	E	F	G	H	I
33	A	B	C	D	E	F	G	H	I
34	A	B	C	D	E	F	G	H	I
35	A	B	C	D	E	F	G	H	I

Exam tip

The more you read, the more the words you will learn. The more words you know, the easier this Reading Paper will be.

Use this page to make a note of new words you come across when you are reading. It will help you remember them if you also write them down in context – that is, in the phrase or sentence that they occur in.

New words	Words in their context

Acknowledgements

The Publishers are grateful to the following for permission to reproduce copyright material:

Orange Telecommunications for the use of their Advertisement on page 6; BLA Group for the article 'Romance on the Railways' taken from *XC Magazine* issue 5 on page 10, and an article on various schools taken from *20:20 Magazine* 6/7/1996 on page 54; North West Water for the use of their Advertisement on page 16; Neil Richardson for the extracts from *Streets Away from Paradise – Reminiscences of a Stalybridge Lad* by Eli Hague on pages 31 and 58; *The Daily Telegraph* for the article 'The Courage to Ride Against All the Odds' by Jessica Davis, DT 14/11/1995, reproduced by permission of Ewan MacNaughton Associates, on page 32; Premier Magazine Group for the articles on four British airports, first published in British Airways *High Life Magazine*, on page 38; *Business Traveller* for the article 'A Cookery Course' by Andy Gill, September 1995 © Business Traveller, on page 57; Examination sample answer sheet reproduced by permission of the University of Cambridge Local Examinations Syndicate on page 84.

Every effort has been made to trace copyright holders and to obtain their permission for the use of copyright material, including:

an article from Waterstone's (Manchester) *Newsletter* on page 5; an article from *Airside*, Manchester Airport's Business News on page 5; an article 'Music to Help Your Brain' from the *Daily Telegraph* 23/3/1996 on page 8; an article 'Making Better Use of Time at Work' from the *Manchester Evening News* 26/1/1996 on page 9; an extract 'A Sad Ending Becomes a Happy Ending' from the Royal Exchange Theatre Manchester's programme to *Carousel* on page 12; an extract from the Lathkill Dale Hotel's brochure on page 16; an extract from *Soap Box* by H. Kingsley published by MacMillan on page 19; an extract from *Forbidden Science* by R. Milton published by Fourth Estate on page 20; an extract from *My Oedipus Complex* by F. O'Connor published by Penguin on page 23; a Qantas Advertisement on page 28; an article from the Manchester Cornerhouse brochure on page 46; an article 'Problem for Students' from the *Manchester Evening News* on page 49; an extract 'The Irish Language Today' from *Ireland and the Irish* by John Ardagh published by Penguin on page 50; an article 'A Lucky Passenger' from the *Daily Telegraph* 24/10/1995 on page 60.

The author and publishers will gladly receive any information enabling them to rectify any error or omission in subsequent editions.